Stage One
Riding & Stable Management

Re dhead

Stage One - Riding & Stable Management

First published in Great Britain by Nova Publications, 1995.
Reprinted 1995
Reprinted 1996
Reprinted 1998

Nova Publications,
Olive House, 22, Frys Lane, Yateley, Hants., GU46 7TJ, United Kingdom.
Tel - (+44) 01252 874981

ISBN 0 9525859 0 1
British Library Cataloguing in Publication Data.
A Catalogue record for this book is available from the British Library.

Typeset in Yateley by Dreke.
Printed and bound by Intype, Input Typesetting Ltd., Wimbledon.

Illustrations by Hazel Reed and Tracey Humphreys.
Computer Graphics by Hazel Reed.

Contents

Foreword

This book deals systematically with the requirements for the BHS Stage One examination in a clear, comprehensive and practical way. It will prove a valuable reference book for all students.

It is often difficult to find all the relevant information for an examination in one book, but I feel the authors have achieved this. The information offered is further enhanced by the friendly manner in which it has been written.

This book will have a place for all students whether embarking on a career with horses or wishing purely to further their knowledge of horsemastership.

Valerie Lee

Valerie Lee, BHSI
Chief Examiner.

Acknowledgements

We would like to thank all those persons who made this project possible; Caroline Lycett, BHSII.BHSSM (Registered), Jamie Whitehorn, Diane Salt BHSAI, Ian Spalding, Tracey Humphreys, Andrea Hinks, Bronia Hill, BHSII (Registered), Jackie Shaw, Jackie Penny, Rachel Mabere BHSAI, Gina and Bob Kendall. Thanks also to Derek Reed and Jamie Whitehorn for all their tremendous help as back up support on the Computer.

We would also like to express our gratitude to all those who gave *their* time so that we could spend *our* time writing, namely my husband Derek, my children Sophie, Martyn and Helena.

Thanks also to Mr. & Mrs. J Sayers at Perrybridge Farm, Sandhurst, Berks for allowing us to photograph at their Livery Yard and to Mr. & Mrs. W. Hundley, Rycroft School of Equitation, Eversley, Hants.

A special thank you to Sharon Sayers who is an absolute angel.

We dedicate this book to some great equine characters, Sue, Autumn Beauty, Harry, Bella and Murphy.

Note: We do apologize to all fillies and mares for the use throughout of the male gender. We wanted to avoid using 'it' as this sounds impersonal. 'He or she' makes the text difficult to read. 'He', 'his' or 'him', with respect, refers to all horses and ponies everywhere.

Cover Photograph by David Hart. Taken at Rycroft School of Equitation, a BHS Examination Centre, with the kind permission of Mr. & Mrs. W. Hundley.

Introduction

There are many excellent books on riding and horse care but, at the time of writing, no specific book that covers each British Horse Society Stage Examination. We wanted to create a series of books which exclusively and comprehensively cover the 'Stages'. This series starts with the 'Stage I' and is followed by 'The Riding and Road Safety Test & Stage II' and 'The Preliminary Teaching Test & Stage III'. These guides give all the information required for each particular exam, drastically reducing the need for a vast library of books.

Each guide in the series has a 'cut off point' giving sufficient information to take students up to the level required for that particular exam. It is often difficult for students to decide exactly how much to learn for each stage, particularly when most books delve deeply into specific aspects of horse care. These Guides provide information which will enable students and their lecturers to prepare for the exams with confidence.

Purpose of the Stage I Guide

The purpose of this Guide is to encourage all those who own, ride or work with horses, to enter and pass the BHS Stage One Examination. Anyone interested in horses and ponies can gain a personal achievement through their experience and study, whether it is for a career or just out of the pure love of equestrianism.

The Guide details the Stage I syllabus, describing the theoretical and practical knowledge the student will require to enter and pass the Examination. Included in the text are aids for learning and memorizing relevant points as well as exam tips and information gained from personal experiences.

Whilst each subject is comprehensively covered, the text includes basic information. This is for two reasons. Firstly, experience has proved that in the assumption that students have a basic knowledge, it is the simplest facts that are often overlooked. Secondly, the more knowledgeable student can use these elementary sections as revision.

The riding section covers the technical knowledge needed for the Stage I examination. Examples of movements and figures are included and can be practised in a school under the auspices of a BHS instructor. Whilst there are many excellent instructors who are not BHS qualified, the importance of good training with a BHS instructor cannot be over emphasized.

As well as being instructive, we hope this guide will be enjoyable. There are times when humour can emphasize important points or facts, helping us to remember and understand their relevance. Working with and caring for horses is a dedicated profession and, whilst many aspects are serious especially with regard to safety, we believe that learning about horses should be enjoyed. By whichever means we increase our knowledge, this will eventually benefit horses and ponies improving their care and well-being.

C H A P T E R   1
General Information

Passing the Stage I is, for those wishing to make a career with horses, the first step to gaining a British Horse Society qualification and a personal achievement for those who ride as a recreation. The training offers a structured approach to learning about horses both in riding and care, covering a wide variety of subjects. For all students the Stage I is a comprehensive introduction to the world of equestrianism.

Eligibility

All applicants for the Stage I must be:

- A member of the British Horse Society at the time of application and on the day of the examination.

- 16 years or over.

The Syllabus

The exam is divided into two main sections - Riding and Horse Knowledge/Care. The Horse Knowledge section is split into Theory, Practical and Practical Oral sessions.

Riding.

For the Stage I the examiners are assessing the rider's knowledge and capability in the basic principles of equitation.

General Assess the horse's tack for fitting and condition - check and tighten the girth from the ground - lead a fully tacked horse in hand at trot and walk - mount and dismount correctly from the ground and from a mounting block - help other riders to mount by assisting from a mounting block or by giving a leg up - check and alter stirrups - check and tighten the girth when mounted.

Equitation   A correct, balanced position at walk, trot and canter - at rising and sitting trot - without stirrups at walk and trot. The correct basic techniques when performing simple school figures and when asking the horse for transitions from one pace to another - how to halt and keep the horse still in halt. The ability to ride the horse forwards in all paces - an elementary understanding of how the horse moves - knowledge of diagonals at trot and the ability to ride on the correct diagonal - the correct leading leg in canter and the ability to ask for the correct leading leg.

Safety   Knowledge of school commands and etiquette - an awareness of other riders and the ability to maintain safe distances from other horses.

Horse Knowledge and Care

The assessment for this section is based on the practical experience and knowledge that the candidate shows.

General   The correct method of approaching and handling horses - the principle of correction and reward for discipline - knowledge and practical experience of working under supervision with horses in the stable and at grass. Understanding the importance of physical fitness and the general principles of yard work - care and use of stable equipment - a sensible, caring attitude to horses and to fellow workers.

Psychology   Knowledge and experience of the horse's characteristics and instincts - how the horse reacts in different environments - how to handle the horse safely and the need for calmness, competence and confidence in handling.

Anatomy   The points of the horse - the main external areas - colours and markings.

Health   Recognising and describing the signs of good or ill health for horses and ponies in the stable and at grass - why an immediate report is essential.

General Management
Basic daily routine and why this is essential. Knowledge and practical experience of fitting, putting on, and leading a horse in a headcollar - how and where to tie a horse up safely - how to stand a horse up correctly for inspection or shoeing. Grooming procedures, equipment and the importance of grooming. How to fill, weigh and tie up a haynet.

Bedding   Types of bedding, advantages and disadvantages - mucking out and bedding down - setting fair stable and yard. Care of muck heaps.

Watering	Rules and considerations of watering - methods of watering in the stable and the field.
Feeding	Aims, rules and considerations of feeding - types of feed and their basic values - cooked feed - amounts to feed horses and ponies in light work. Types of hay and their respective values.
Saddlery	The Snaffle Bridle - points of the bridle - fitting and condition - different types of snaffle bit - different nosebands. The General Purpose saddle - points of the saddle - fitting and condition. Numnahs and saddle cloths. Care, cleaning and storage of saddlery.
Clothing	Types of rugs and their uses - putting on, fitting and taking off rugs correctly. Care, cleaning and storage of rugs.
Shoeing	The horse's foot - importance of regular shoeing - recognising when the horse needs shoeing and signs of good shoeing.

Grassland Management

> Field inspections and maintenance - recognising good and bad pasture - turning out and bringing in the horse correctly. Safety in the field.

General Knowledge

> Safety precautions - in the stable - the yard - when riding in the countryside and on the public highway. Accident procedures. The aims of the British Horse Society.

BHS Examination Structure

The BHS Stage I is the first of a progressive series of examinations. Students who pass the Riding and Horse Knowledge sections in Stage I, II and III, the Riding and Road Safety Test, the Preliminary Teaching Test and teach for the appropriate number of hours will be awarded the Assistant Instructor's Certificate.

If the student has also obtained a First Aid certificate to Health and Safety at work standard, he or she will be eligible for inclusion into the British Horse Society's list of registered instructors. They will be entitled to put after their name, BHSAI (Reg'd).

The Riding and Horse Knowledge sections may be taken separately in all the stage examinations. Passing the Horse Knowledge and Care section up to Stage III will allow the successful student to gain the BHS Groom's Certificate.

There are further qualifications to be gained after the AI or the Grooms Certificate; the BHS Intermediate Instructor qualification, the full Instructor Certificate and the ultimate qualification; the Fellowship of the British Horse Society.

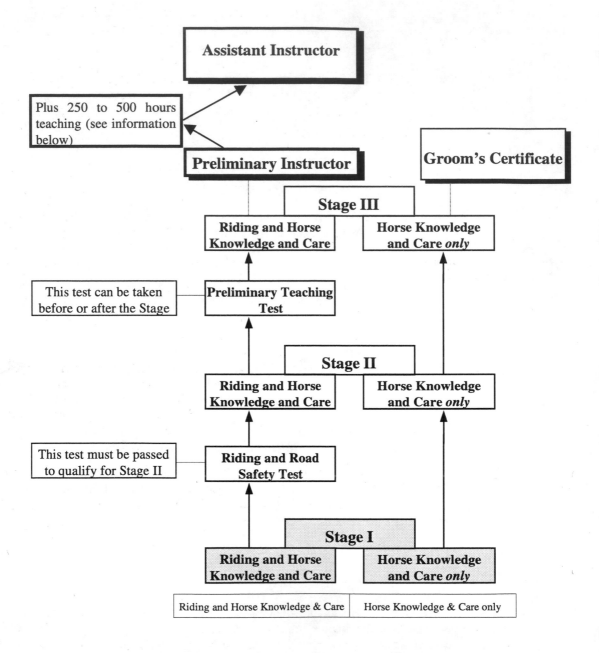

Figure 1: Table of BHS Qualifications up to Assistant Instructor level

New structure

From January 1st 1996 a new structure was introduced. All those passing the Stage exams, the Riding and Road Safety and the Preliminary Teaching tests, will be awarded the Preliminary Teacher's certificate.

To achieve an Assistant Instructors certificate, Preliminary Teachers must gain at least 250 hours teaching experience within a BHS 'Where to train' centre (listed in the 'Where to train' book). Those who teach at other establishments need 500 hours. Freelance instructors, teaching at various centres, will be able to count one hour as two when they teach at a 'Where to train' centre. Some of the hours required may be offset by attending teaching courses given by the British Horse Society.

The Escorts' Exam

Another examination that has been introduced is the Riding Escort Certificate. This tests candidates on their competency to take charge of a hack and is designed for those in charge of clients riding out in the countryside and on the road. It aims to promote a more efficient escort who is knowledgeable about safety precautions and first aid. Details for this may be obtained from the British Horse Society. *This examination does not constitute part of the requirements for the AI qualification.*

Where to train

The best place to train is at a BHS Approved riding school. Here working pupils will be given formal training and private students can choose to have riding and stable management lessons when available. Each BHS approved establishment is regularly inspected and assessed so that it can offer a level of teaching to a specified standard. The BHS book on Approved Establishments lists the schools and centres in the UK and describes the standard to which each school can train candidates.

There are also a number of colleges offering courses which will take the student up to Assistant Instructor level and beyond. Most colleges offer comprehensive courses which, with equestrian studies, include training for business, secretarial and GCSE 'A' level qualifications. These advertise regularly in equestrian magazines and are usually excellent value.

Proficiency Tests

As an introduction to the BHS examination format there are the Proficiency tests. These are **not compulsory** for students of the Stage I and are aimed mostly at the recreational rider. They are an excellent preparation for the BHS stages especially for children or the less confident adult. These short tests, which subdivide the riding and horse care categories into smaller sections, are conducted and assessed internally by the Riding School at which they are held. Details of the Proficiency tests can be obtained from most BHS Approved Establishments.

Preparation for the Exam

Students should practise all the exercises expected in the riding section. Even the simple exercises such as mounting, checking and altering stirrups and girths need to be performed in a safe and correct way. This will create a confidence that will be of tremendous help during the examination.

Having lessons in a BHS approved Riding School, in an indoor school or menage with other riders and being instructed by a BHS qualified instructor is of paramount importance. A rider who is not used to school commands or rules and who is confused by riding school figures with others will find the exam difficult. This will be a pity, particularly if the rider has good riding ability.

For the Horse Knowledge, students need to study from relevant literature (this book!), to attend lectures at an Approved establishment and to gain personal experience in the practical aspects of stable management.

With good preparation, regular instruction, a reasonable physical fitness and a willingness to learn, the Stage I is well within the reach of all students.

Note: though correct at going to press, and whilst every effort is made to keep these books up to date, the contents of the syllabus can change at any time. Candidates are always advised to contact the British Horse Society or the Examination Centre prior to their Exam to discover if any alterations or additions have been made.

Note: The equitation in the Stage One is being revised and slightly restructured as from 1999. It is planned to include work over ground (trotting) poles with riders showing a slightly forward seat. This is to assess the rider's position and balance over poles, and as a preliminary to jumping.

The forward position is used in jumping to maintain the balance of both horse and rider. The rider may use a *slightly* forward position over poles to allow the horse freedom of movement.

The rider folds from the hips bringing the shoulders into a position in line with the knees. The seat is brought slightly away from the saddle. The rider maintains the balance through the suppleness of the hip, knee and ankle joints, and by keeping the weight down the leg into the heel.

C H A P T E R   2
Equitation

Training for the Stage I provides a solid basis on which to progress to more advanced riding. The rider is taught, and will learn to acquire, the suppleness and co-ordination needed to gain an effective, balanced position at the three basic paces of walk, trot and canter.

This chapter outlines the requirements needed for the rider at the Stage I level and describes the examination format; dealing with the school figures and exercises that the rider will need to know. Though the techniques of riding can only be taught in practical terms with a qualified instructor, some of the basic points are given here to help the student and to act as a revision prior to the exam.

General Preparation

The importance of good quality instruction from the very start is essential. This is particularly so with respect to riding. If the correct techniques are taught from the beginning they will last a lifetime and be a foundation on which to build and progress. Bad habits that are allowed to creep in during the basic stages will be incredibly difficult to overcome later. It is worth finding a good qualified instructor from the beginning.

Lessons on the lunge are excellent for teaching balance and for strengthening and deepening the seat. Some time spent riding without stirrups also teaches balance, supples the hip joint and stretches the muscles and tendons in the legs. This exercise should only be performed for short periods or until the rider tires. After this the value is lost as the rider tenses and grips.

Once the riding position has been established, (and most people deciding to take their Stage I have been riding for some time), the rider continues to learn by performing school figures and by improving the quality of the horse's paces and transitions.

The rider needs to learn to ride safely with others and to follow the commands given by the Instructor. This knowledge can only be gained from practical experience; taking lessons with other riders in a school or menage. The student for the Stage I should also ride a variety of horses. This will increase the awareness and adaptability of the rider. The owner/rider who only rides one horse will find it very difficult to cope with two or three 'school' horses on the exam day.

Basic Principles of Equitation

The Rider's Position

The rider sits in the deepest part of the saddle with an even weight on both seat bones. The thighs and knees lie softly against the saddle with the lower legs touching the horse's sides. The feet point forwards with the heel slightly lower than the toe. With the leg in position the stirrup leather should hang down vertically from the stirrup bar.

The back is held straight and the ribcage lifted; the shoulders level and relaxed. The upper arms lie lightly by the rider's side with the elbows bent. The hands are held level with the lower arms and hands forming a straight line from the elbow to bit. The reins are held with the thumb on top and the fingers encircling the rein with the tips flat against the palm of the hand. The hand should not make a fist or clench the reins tightly.

The head faces forward and the rider looks towards the direction of travel. The head should not tilt to either side or be bowed with the rider looking at the ground.

The whole position, whilst held straight, should be one of controlled relaxation. The rider will then be capable of applying the aids correctly and effectively.

The Aids

The aids are the method by which the rider communicates with the horse; the language through which the rider asks the horse to act. There are two types of aid - the natural and the artificial. The natural aids are the *legs*, *seat and body*, *hands* and *voice*. The main artificial aids are the *whip* and *spurs*.

When referring to aids, the terms 'inside' and 'outside' are often used. The **'inside'** is the *side to which the horse is bent*. Though this usually means the inside of the school or a circle, because the horse is bending that way, in some more advanced movements the horse is bent away from the inside of the school. Similarly the **'outside'** is the side away from the bend of the horse.

The **'bend'** of a horse is the way in which his body is curved. On a circle to the right the horse will have a right 'bend', circling to the left he will have a left 'bend'.

The Natural Aids

The aids are used in conjunction with each other and by co-ordinating the leg and hand aids the rider asks for energy and maintains the desired pace. The aids should only be used when necessary; *at all other times the rider should sit as quietly as possible.*

The Legs

The legs ask for energy, bend and forward movement or, in more advanced riding, sideways movement. The leg aids are applied by increasing the pressure against the horse's side in a squeezing action either in the region of the girth or for some movements slightly behind the girth.

The Seat and Body

The seat and body aids are used more as the rider progresses into advanced riding. At this level the rider should sit in balance with the horse, learning to feel and be in 'tune' with his movements.

The Hands

The hands should always be used in conjunction with other aids; the legs or the seat and body. They control the direction and speed of the horse by a 'squeeze and relax' action on the reins.

The Voice

This aid is used mainly when training and lungeing horses. The use of the voice is not encouraged when performing flatwork and is penalised in dressage tests when the horse is expected to respond to the other aids. There are times though when the rider can use the voice to encourage, pacify, reprimand or praise the horse when necessary.

Artificial Aids

The Whip

The whip is used to discipline the horse if he does not respect the leg aid. If a horse constantly refuses to respond to the leg aids he must be reprimanded or he will continue to ignore the rider. This will result in a sluggish, unresponsive horse. If the horse does not respond to the leg, the aid is repeated and at the same time the whip is used behind that leg to reinforce the aid. With a short whip this does mean the rider has to take a hand off the reins.

When riding in a school or menage, the whip is normally carried in the inside hand to back up the leg asking for impulsion. The whip needs to be transferred to the new inside hand when changing the rein. The whip is passed from one hand to another *after* the new rein is established; this will prevent the horse shying away from the whip at a difficult moment.

The Spurs

This artificial aid is not permitted in the Stage I. When used for more advanced riding spurs are applied lightly for a more immediate response to a gentler aid. They should not be jabbed into the horse's side to strengthen the leg.

The Three Basic Paces

Each pace, walk, trot and canter, has its own beat or series of footfalls; the sequence in which the horse's feet touch the ground. The rhythm of each movement depends on the regularity of the beat.

The Walk

This has a four-time beat with each foot touching the ground at different times; left hind, left fore, right hind and right fore. The horse should walk actively as though he is marching, with a definite 1-2-3-4 rhythm.

Figure 2: Footfalls at walk, feet touching the ground at different times.

LH/LF = left or **near** hind and fore. RH/RF = right or **off** hind and fore

The Trot

This is a two-time beat with the diagonal feet touching the ground in a 1-2, 1-2 rhythm; for instance, right fore and left hind then left fore and right hind.

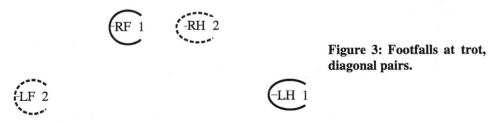

Figure 3: Footfalls at trot, diagonal pairs.

To help the horse move freely and balance himself the rider rises to the trot; sitting for one beat and rising for the alternate beat. In the school the horse's inside hind leg takes most of the weight of both horse and rider. The rider sits when the inside hind is on the ground and rises when it is lifted, to allow the forward movement. This is called being on the 'correct diagonal'.

When the rein is changed the diagonal is also changed by the rider sitting for two consecutive beats. When crossing the school or riding serpentines the rider changes the diagonal in the centre of the school or on the centre line. When riding a half circle and inclining back to the track, the diagonal is changed on reaching the track.

The Canter

This is a three-time beat with a hind leg pushing into canter, followed by a diagonal pair and then a fore. For instance when cantering to the left the right hind strikes off first, followed by the diagonal pair of left hind/right fore and lastly the left fore (the leading leg). For canter to the right - the left hind strikes off, followed by right hind/left fore and finally the right fore.

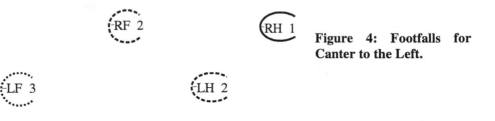

Figure 4: Footfalls for Canter to the Left.

Variations in pace

There are variations within each movement - walk may be collected, medium, extended and free; trot may be collected, working, medium and extended and canter can be collected, working, medium and extended. In addition to the three paces the horse's fourth natural gait is gallop. For the Stage I the rider is required to ride at medium walk, working trot and working canter.

Transitions

This is a change from one pace to another or from one variation of a pace to another, for example working trot to medium trot. An upward transition is from a slower to a faster pace and a downward transition from a faster to a slower pace. A transition made from one pace to the next is called progressive - walk to trot. A transition made from one pace to another out of sequence is called direct - walk to canter. (Riders will not be required to ride a direct transition in the Stage I.)

Good transitions are important to keep the horse and rider in balance and to ensure that the new pace is active and in rhythm. Transitions should be smooth with the horse going forwards (even in downward transitions).

The important point to remember with all transitions is the **preparation**. First the horse must be moving actively and going forward. Then, a few strides before the transition, the rider prepares the horse by slightly increasing the pressure of the legs whilst at the the same time, squeezing and relaxing the hand on the outside rein. This is the basic 'half-halt' which balances and prepares the horse in readiness for the change of pace. This preparation is especially vital for downward transitions to prevent the horse from suddenly dropping or falling into the slower pace.

The half-halt should be a subtle and almost invisible signal between rider and horse. It should be applied softly but effectively without restricting the horse's forward movement.

Upward transitions

For halt to walk and walk to trot, the rider increases the pressure of the legs equally and allows the forward movement with the hands. For the transition trot to canter, the trot must be active **but not fast**; springing rather than racing. The rider sits to the trot a few strides before the transition point. The inside hand squeezes the rein to indicate the direction of travel; the outside hand remains steady to keep the trot rhythm and tempo. The inside leg aid is applied on the girth and the outside leg aid slightly behind the girth.

Downward Transitions

The rider sits a little deeper into the saddle keeping the seat 'soft'. The outside hand aid is applied with a squeeze and relax action whilst the inside hand remains in contact and still. The legs are kept in contact with the horse's side to maintain the impulsion throughout the transition.

The Halt

The horse at halt should ideally stand evenly and squarely on all four legs. The rider achieves this during the transition from walk by maintaining impulsion with the legs evenly and by squeezing and relaxing both hands with equal pressure. The rider should then sit quietly and evenly in the saddle to maintain the halt.

Turns and Circles

These are used to change direction, to vary the movements within the school and to supple, stretch and build up the horse's muscles. To perform a correct turn or circle the horse must be balanced and 'straight'. It sounds a contradiction in terms to be 'straight on a circle' but this straightness refers to the 'line' through the horse's body from poll to tail. This should be a direct, constant line. When this is achieved the horse's hind feet will step on the same 'line' as the corresponding fore feet.

For the horse to achieve this the rider must sit centrally in the saddle, with the inside shoulder slightly behind the outside shoulder. Try walking a circle at home and look to see where the inside shoulder is in relation to the outside shoulder. Now try walking the circle with the inside shoulder in front of the outside shoulder; this is much more difficult.

To maintain the line on a turn or circle the rider increases the pressure of the inside leg on the girth encouraging bend. If the horse's outside shoulder starts to drift, the outside hand squeezes the rein to regain the curve.

The turn most frequently ridden badly is the turn at each corner of the school. The horse must be encouraged to bend himself into the corners by the use of the rider's inside leg, which sometimes needs applying quite firmly.

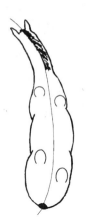

Figure 5: Horse on Turn.

Figure 6: Horse on Circle.

The Stage One Examination

This part of the chapter follows the exam format giving descriptions of exercises and figures required in the syllabus.

The candidates will be divided into groups and each group will be taken in turn to the school for the riding session. Once in the school each rider will be allocated a horse and asked to check the horse's tack for fitting and condition. (See the chapters dealing with Saddlery.)

The examiners will then request that the riders lead their horse in hand at walk and trot. Each rider should make sure that they take the horse out and allow themselves plenty of room for leading and for the turn at the end of the school.

Leading a saddled and bridled horse in hand

Check that the saddle is secure first, if necessary by tightening the girth. The stirrups are made safe.

For greater security the loop of the stirrup leather can be taken under the bottom of the iron and placed behind the leather in the centre.

The end of the leather is then passed through the loop and secured.

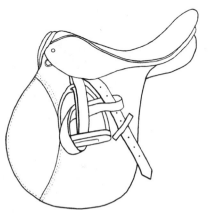

Figure 7: One method of securing the stirrups.

If there is no martingale attachment to the bridle, the reins are taken from the horse's neck, over his head and held near the horse's mouth with the right hand, if leading from the left. The reins are separated by the index finger. The buckle end, together with the whip, is held in the left hand and the horse led from the position of his shoulder. The rider should not exert any pressure on the horse's mouth through the bit.

For horses wearing a martingale, the reins remain on the neck. The reins are held in the right hand near the bit with the index finger separating them. The whip is held in the left hand.

Each rider must make sure that the horse is moving actively and is turned correctly with the rider on the outside. (See chapter on Headcollars for turning.) The examiners will be assessing the movement and action of the horse and the control the handler shows when leading.

Whilst the horse is normally led from the near or left side, there are circumstances when he must be led from the offside. For example, a handler leading a horse on the road does so on the offside, between the horse and the traffic. Here the reins are held in the left hand under the chin, the whip and buckle end of the reins in the right.

After the leading in hand the riders will be requested to mount, check the girths and adjust stirrups.

Mounting and dismounting from the ground

A horse is normally mounted and dismounted on the left or nearside, a tradition dating from the days when swords were worn as part of everyday dress. With the sword on the left side of the body, mounting and dismounting on the nearside prevented the sword from becoming tangled up with the rider's legs.

Mounting

Check the girth first and tighten if necessary. Pull the stirrup irons down the leathers gently; snapping the irons down can not only startle the horse but will weaken the leathers by stretching them and stripping the surface. The stirrups can be checked for approximate length by placing one hand at the top of the leather on the stirrup bar. The stirrup is held up against this stretched arm; the iron should just reach the armpit.

Taking both reins and the whip in the left hand, hold these on top of the horse's neck just in front of the withers. The reins should be sufficiently short to prevent the horse from moving off. The right rein should be a little shorter so that if the horse does move whilst the rider has one foot in the stirrup, the horse's body will swing towards the rider and not away leaving the rider frantically hopping to catch up.

Facing the horse's hindquarters twist the stirrup iron clockwise and place the left foot in the stirrup with the toe pointing down. Turn on the right foot to face the saddle and place the right hand over in front of the cantle. The cantle should not be pulled on to mount as this will drag it across the horse's spine. Hop on the right leg and push up lifting the leg well over the horse's hindquarters. The seat is lowered gently and quietly into the saddle.

If the horse has behaved and stayed still he will deserve a pat. It is easy to forget that this living animal has just stood and allowed a rider to mount on his back. A reward will encourage him to stand correctly in future.

Checking and altering stirrups when mounted

Once mounted the rider can check the length of stirrup by removing both feet from the irons. The legs should be allowed to hang freely by the horse's sides. The bottom of the stirrup should just reach the ankle bone. In the Stage I it is a common mistake for riders to try and ride with their stirrups too long, believing that this will automatically deepen the seat. At this level it is more likely to weaken it as the rider will try and reach for the irons and become insecure in the saddle. It is wiser to begin with the stirrups a little shorter and to lengthen them later.

When altering the stirrups the feet are put back into the irons and remain there whilst the length is changed. When the length is correct the end of the leather can be placed in the surcingle loop of the saddle if there is one. The position of the foot in the stirrup can also be checked and corrected if necessary. The widest part of the foot should rest on the bar of the stirrup with the iron at right angles to the foot.

Checking and adjusting girths

The girth should always be checked again after a few minutes of riding when it is likely to need adjusting. The girth can be tightened at walk. If the horse is touchy about his girth area or the girth is difficult to alter, the rider should come into the centre of the school and halt to make adjustments. The girth is sufficiently tight when there is just enough room for the flat of the hand to slide between the girth and the horse's side.

Riding without stirrups at walk and trot

When everyone is ready the instructor will ask the ride to walk to the track. The riders must act *as a ride* with the leader keeping an eye on those behind and everyone maintaining their correct distances - one horse's length between each horse. It is quite in order for a rider to turn across a corner to catch the ride up if this is necessary.

At some point the riders will be asked to halt, quit, cross the stirrups and to ride at walk and trot without stirrups.

When quitting and crossing the stirrups, pull the buckle down well clear of the stirrup bar, twist the leather so that the buckle is underneath and place the stirrup and leather over in front of the saddle. The right stirrup is crossed over first so that if the rider has to dismount the left stirrup, placed on top, can easily be let down for the rider to mount. The Stage I rider should be capable of riding correctly and comfortably without stirrups for at least 15 to 20 minutes.

The riders will then be asked to take back their stirrups, halt on the centre line, dismount and change horses.

Dismounting

The reins and whip are held in the left hand and the right hand placed on the pommel. Both feet are removed from the stirrups. The rider leans forward and the right leg is lifted well over the horse's hindquarters. The rider lands gently on both feet beside the horse's shoulder.

Riders will now be asked give another rider a leg up or assist from a mounting block.

The Leg Up

This needs practising before the exam with riders of varying heights and weights, using horses of different sizes.

The rider and person assisting should agree first on the timing. Some riders prefer to mount on the count of three whilst others prefer a count of three and then 'up'. It is extremely difficult trying to lift a rider who is not ready!

One important point of which to be aware, is the whip. This should be held in the left hand on the OFFSIDE shoulder of the horse. If held on the nearside it has a tendency to rise up and hit the person assisting in the face. It should also be kept still so that it does not hit the horse.

The rider holds the reins sufficiently short so that the horse does not move forwards (but not so tight that the horse moves backwards). The *right* rein is held a little shorter as in mounting.

The rider's left leg is bent and the assistant, keeping a straight back, holds this leg in both hands. The rider hops whilst counting and pushes up at the agreed moment. At precisely that moment the assistant lifts. The rider should land on the saddle *quietly and gently*, not with a great thump.

Mounting from a block

If the rider is to mount from the ground or a mounting block, the person assisting should stand on the offside of the horse. The assistant holds the reins near the horse's mouth in the right hand, whilst holding the stirrup steady with the left.

This time the rider should hold the whip in the left hand on the *nearside* of the horse. (A whip should never be held in the right hand when mounting from the left, as it will end up being sat on!). Always thank the assistant when finished.

Figure 8: The Leg Up.

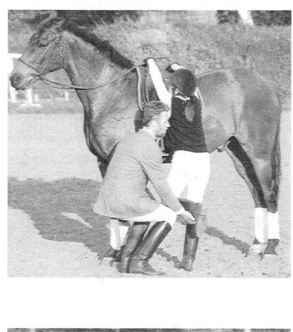

Equitation

Each rider will ride two or, at the discretion of the Chief Examiner, three different horses. Part of the session will be performed as a 'ride' and part in 'open order' with riders working individually. Riders will be requested to perform simple school figures at walk, trot (rising and sitting) and canter on both reins; to quit and cross the stirrups and to ride without stirrups at walk and trot. The Examiners are looking for a **firm, secure seat** that does not interfere with the horse.

School Figures

School figures are the manoeuvres performed within the school such as turns, circles and changes of rein. To help the rider practise and prepare for the Stage I, examples are given for school figures and exercises that may be requested during the examination.

Figure 9: Plan of a School.

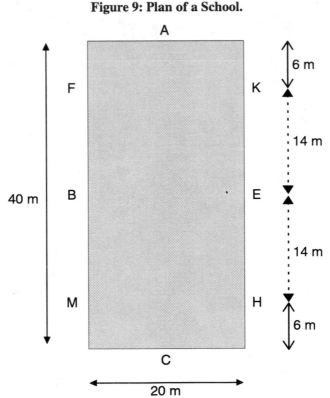

School figures that may be required during the Exam

1.   Twenty metre circles at walk, trot and canter.

2.   Fifteen metre circles at trot.

Figure 10: Circles - showing ten, fifteen and twenty metre circles at B and at A.

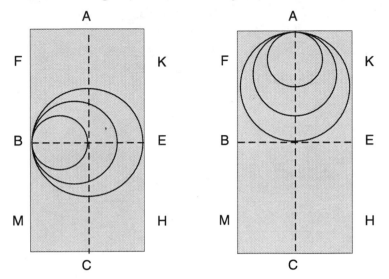

3.   Ten metre circles at trot.

4.   Half twenty metre circles across the school at canter.

Figure 11: A 3 loop serpentine from A on the left rein, each loop going to the wall.

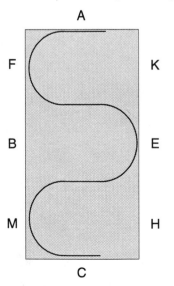

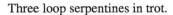

5.   Three loop serpentines in trot.

6.   Turns to the left and right.

Figure 12: Changing rein on short diagonal.   **Figure 13: Changing rein from B to E or vice versa.**

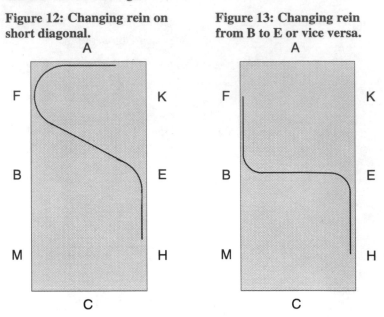

7.   Halting and keeping the halt position.

8.   Changing the rein across a long diagonal, across a short diagonal, up the centre line, by a half circle incline back to the track, across the school from E to B.

Figure 14: Half circle and incline back to track (Demi Volte).

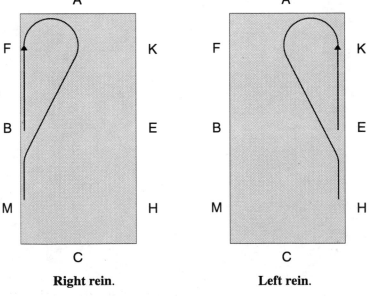

Right rein.   **Left rein.**

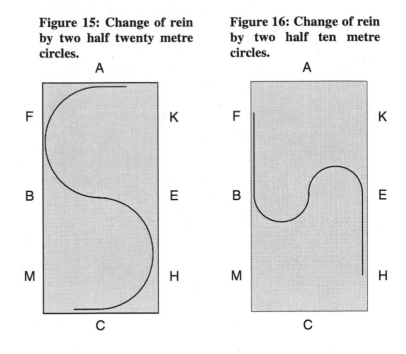

Figure 15: Change of rein by two half twenty metre circles.

Figure 16: Change of rein by two half ten metre circles.

Example of school exercises

These are examples of the type of instructions that will be given to the ride, either by an Examiner or the Instructor in charge.

- Whole ride go forward to walk and track left or right when reaching the track.

- Whole ride prepare to trot and go forward to working trot rising. Trot a twenty metre circle and go large after the exercise.

- In trot, with the whole ride following, leading file turn at A or C markers down the centre line. Change the rein and go large after the exercise.

- Leading files in succession take canter at A or C. At the E or B marker canter a half twenty metre circle before joining the rear of the ride.

- With the rest of the ride in walk, leading file only at A or C, proceed to trot and ride a three loop serpentine. Each loop must reach the wall of the school. Join the rear of the ride.

- With the whole ride in walk, the rear file only halt at A or C and stay in halt for 6 seconds. Proceed to walk and when ready go forward to trot. Pass the whole of the ride in trot and take the leading file. When safe go to walk.

- With the rest of the ride in walk, leading file only go forward to trot and when ready canter. Canter a twenty metre circle away from the ride. Go large and make the transitions from canter to trot and trot to walk before joining the rear of the ride. Each leading file to do this movement in succession.

- With ride in trot the leading file will choose a change of rein, whole ride to follow. Leading file only circle and join the rear of the ride. Each leading file in succession to follow this exercise with a different change of rein.

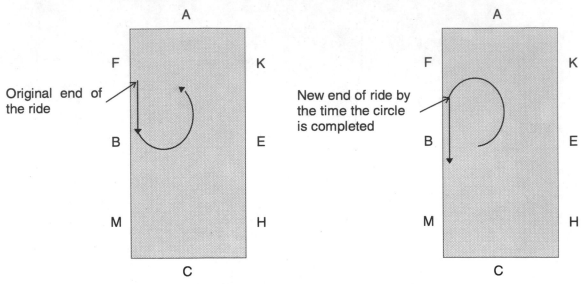

Original end of the ride

New end of ride by the time the circle is completed

Figure 17: The manoeuvre of circling from the front to the rear of the ride.

- Whole ride in trot leading file only turn inwards and halt on the centre line. As the ride passes go forward to trot and join the ride at the rear.

- Whole ride turn inwards and halt on the centre line.

Examiners may often make up their own exercises even sometimes requesting that certain candidates work as individuals, separate from the whole ride.

School commands

There are certain commands that the rider needs to recognise when in the school or menage.

As a ride   All the commands given apply to all the riders in the school.

Leading file   The rider and horse at the front of the ride.

Rear of ride or *rear file*
            The rider and horse at the back.

Open Order   Each rider is equally spaced out around the outer track.

Going large   Riding round the school on the outside track.

Inside or *inner track*
            Riding around the school at about 3 feet inside the outside track.

School Rules

For safety reasons there are also rules for riding in a school with others;

- ***Before entering the school knock and wait for permission to enter.***
  Do not open the door just as a horse is passing or try to lead or ride a horse in the school into the path of another.

- ***Mount and dismount in a safe place.***
  This is usually in the centre of the school.

- ***Correct or safe distance.***
  When riding behind another horse leave a space equivalent to one horse's length.

- ***Left to Left.***
  Riders on different reins pass left hand to left hand.

- ***Faster paces are given priority.***
  When the ride is in open order and riding at different paces, those riding at a faster pace are given the outside track. The rider in walk should come onto an inner track.

- ***Look up around and be aware.***
  Be conscious of the other riders and prepared to avoid a collision.

- ***Before leaving the school ask permission of those still inside.***
  If the door is opened and horses leave, this may cause problems for those riding around the school.

Exam Tip

The most important point to remember throughout the riding session is to *try and relax*. This may prove difficult even if you have trained three of four times a week in this particular school and know the horses well. The minute you enter the door you will be aware of a totally alien atmosphere. There will be two or three examiners sitting in the corner, making notes. The horses may be plaited up waiting in anticipation. There will be other nervous candidates as smartly dressed as you. It all adds to the tension.

Now is the time to take deep breaths, breathing in slowly through the nose and releasing the air from the mouth. Once mounted, release the tension by stretching the legs. Do this quietly whilst altering the stirrups. Let your eyes go 'soft' by relaxing the focus. Shrug your shoulders a few times and gently stretch your neck.

Some fortunate candidates excel in these situations whilst others just tense and become rigid. It can help if you have had the experience of going to shows and competing in dressage tests. It is a very similar situation. If however, this is not possible, train for a few weeks before in the clothes you will wear for the exam. Become used to wearing a shirt, tie and jacket.

Many of the exercises requested in the Stage I need careful timing. When working with four or five other riders, these school figures are not as easy as they appear. It is important that you become used to working in a ride, performing exercises that demand good timing and have the ability to work safely and confidently with others. Particular notice should be taken of the figure circling from the front to the back of the ride. This needs good judgment to enable you to arrive back at the track and rejoin the ride as near as possible at the correct distance behind the last horse. Ideally, too, the trot should be kept at the same pace throughout this manoeuvre. Misjudgment will result in rushing after the ride or slowing the horse down to a walk or even a halt. You need to practise within a school or menage and with a different number of riders as this affects the size of the circle.

Be positive in your thinking, concentrate on what you should do rather than what you should not do. Mistakes can happen but this is not necessarily an automatic failure. If for instance you should discreetly check and discover that you are riding on the wrong diagonal at trot, simply change this in the normal manner by sitting for two beats. For canter on the wrong leg come quietly back to trot; wait until a corner and make the transition to canter again. If the horse continues to lead with the wrong leg, it may be that he has a problem and is a little one-sided. No need to panic, the examiners will realize there is a problem. You may afterwards be asked specifically about the canter aids.

Occasionally at the end of the riding session the Examiner may question candidates about certain points, for instance the aids, their use and application for specific movements. Candidates may have to describe the aids for transitions, turns and circles. It is worth practising this before the exam with your instructor so that you are able to give comprehensive yet clear and concise explanations.

Actions to avoid

Some situations must be avoided and, without dwelling on these, it is wise to be aware of them. Avoid at all costs riding too close to another horse or of cutting up other riders, that is, riding directly across their path. Whilst in open order, do not make a downward transition on the outside track, unless you are requested to do so. Ride onto an inner track or to the centre of the school and make the transition.

Do not ride constantly on the wrong diagonal or in canter on the wrong leading leg. Always check discreetly. Do not let the horse hare round at a pace that suits him so that it appears you have no control.

Though these problems may seem too obvious and simple, it is amazing how even the best riders make silly mistakes on an exam day. Remember, the Examiners do understand about nerves and will always try to give each candidate the benefit of the doubt.

CHAPTER 3
Horse Management

For the Horse Knowledge and Care sections the Stage I student requires an elementary knowledge of horsemastership that, whilst not in any great depth, must be wide and varied. It includes handling the horse in the stable and field and basic practical stable management. The BHS system encourages experience and understanding about the normal daily jobs, the study of theoretical subjects and, most importantly, safety in all aspects of horse care.

The Theory session normally takes place in a separate room. The format will be a mixture of individual questioning and general group discussion on such subjects as psychology, watering and feeding. During the Practical session, candidates are requested to do tasks as individuals such as tacking a horse up and grooming. These are then checked by an examiner. The Practical Oral includes such subjects as points of the horse, colours and markings. This can take the form of individual questioning or a group discussion.

General Principles of Horse Management

Good manners, Communication and Discipline

The principles of good manners, communication and discipline are as important when working with people as they are when handling horses. In the Stage I the examiners will not only be assessing candidates on their knowledge and practical experience but also on how candidates react to each other, and to their fellow workers. They are looking for those who are co-operative, helpful and pleasant. Whilst candidates need to be quietly confident, they must also be willing to listen and learn.

Good manners

Just as people react to the way they are treated so horses reflect the way in which they are handled. Horses are not only totally dependent on their handlers, they are also susceptible to their handler's moods and behaviour.

For instance a bad tempered owner or handler will raise a bad tempered horse that could turn vicious, gain a reputation and be treated accordingly.

The horse, too, must learn good manners and for that he needs to be taught how to act correctly. Simple lessons such as; standing still whilst being groomed, picking up his feet for cleaning without fuss and learning to wait until the rider is properly mounted before walking off. All who work with horses must learn to teach a horse good behaviour.

Communication

Handlers also need to learn to be positive and consistent in their teaching. A horse quickly becomes confused if the handler is changeable or unclear in his demands. Therefore, it is necessary to know what to teach and how to teach it and this comes from knowing the correct ways for working with horses and being confident to do so.

Discipline and reward

Discipline is essential when dealing with horses. If corrected when doing wrong and rewarded when right, the horse will soon learn what actions please and will continue to do these. This will lead to a well mannered animal that will be a pleasure to own. Consequently the horse will have a better life.

Horses need disciplining by firm and confident yet kind and sympathetic handling. They are wild animals that, despite having been domesticated and trained for millennia, still possess their basic instincts. Not only can horses be frightened or angry they can also be mischievous and downright wicked! Many dangerous traits are taught by bad handling, incorrect training or lack of discipline. The horse should never be allowed to persist with bad behaviour or he will quickly learn to act in this manner permanently and it will become a habit.

If the horse misbehaves, he should be reprimanded in a firm, slightly raised voice. This usually stops the misconduct. A firm word or sentence with inflection should be enough.

Constant shouting will make the horse irritable and the handler appear bad-tempered or silly. Eventually the reprimand will be ineffective. The horse will become familiar to the raised voice and ignore it.

If a firm vocal correction is not enough the horse may need contact with a sharp tap of the hand on the neck, hindquarters or, if he bites, on the muzzle. This must be given immediately so that the horse understands why he is being corrected.

Once the horse has learnt his lesson and acts in the right way, he should be rewarded by a pat, a kind voice or occasionally a titbit. He will then associate the good behaviour with a pleasant treat. The ideal is to discipline the horse by correction and reward, **correcting bad behaviour, rewarding good.**

All horses are born relatively innocent, for the most part it is the way in which they are handled which encourages good or bad habits and manners. They are friendly, gentle creatures especially towards human beings and with correct care they gain confidence and trust, develop good habits and become very loving.

Handling The Horse

As previously mentioned, the BHS are concerned principally with safety but into this sphere and connected with it, is the manner and method of handling, working with and treating horses.

The horse is a living animal possessing instincts and characteristics that determine the way he reacts. Horses do not logically work things out; they do not think as humans do. In many ways their senses are far more developed and finely tuned, a result of being a victim rather than a predator.

The horse still retains most of its instinctive defensive mechanisms. These are often used to an advantage in handling. Even so, when dealing with horses, it must be remembered that this animal does frequently react in an unpredictable manner causing injury and even death. Awareness is essential at all times, even with familiar and trusted horses or ponies.

Careful, considerate and correct handling is so important for the development of a horse's character. For instance, if a horse's girth is done up quickly pinching his skin or causing pain, he cannot turn round and say 'Excuse me that hurt.' He can only complain by showing his teeth or lifting a leg. His method of communication is limited to facial expression and posture. If the painful action is constantly repeated, the horse becomes desperate and uses his strength to warn and hopefully prevent it.

Approaching a horse in a stable

Relatively speaking a stabled horse is a trapped horse and though most are not affected by this environmental state, it is possible that a nervous, vicious or highly strung animal can react to this situation. Even the most even-tempered horse may resent his privacy being disturbed, especially when eating.

Approach the horse in his box by walking quietly from the front in plain sight. Shouting, running and bouncing up suddenly at the door will only alarm him. Speak softly, perhaps calling the horse's name.

In the case of a strange horse beware of him lunging over the door. Thankfully not many do this but, with an unfamiliar animal, it is better to be safe than sorry.

Sticking a hand or arm over the box to stroke or pat the horse may surprise him. He may, in reaction, lunge at the door or run to the back of the box.

Look to see where the horse is in the box. Keep talking; this not only puts the horse at ease but informs him of your whereabouts. Most horses will turn and come to the doorway, which is the desired result.

If the horse has his hindquarters facing the door do not enter the box, this action may startle him and he may kick. Encourage the horse's head around so that he is able to see you and be aware of your presence.

When the horse is facing the door, undo the bolt and kick bolt quietly. Open the door just wide enough to enter. Some horses if they see an open door do try and rush through it. Move the horse back quietly if necessary, then close the door and fasten the top bolt. If the stable has a chain or pole, fasten this first before opening the door fully.

Once inside the box approach the horse by walking towards his shoulder and neck. Gain control as soon as possible by putting on his headcollar. Continue to talk to him quietly; this will assure him that you are there as a friend and will put him at ease.

How to work around a horse

When working with horses on a daily basis it is easy to become inattentive, particularly if the horse in question is well-mannered. Even the quietest horse may react in an unusual, maybe violent way, at some time and for some reason.

It is safer to work in the box whilst the horse is out, either being exercised, at pasture or tied up outside. This may not always be possible and there are occasions when the horse must stay in the box.

Always restrain the horse with a headcollar and lead rope whilst working with or around him in the stable.

Never try and work in a confined space between the horse and the stable wall. Manoeuvre him with a gentle push on the hindquarters whilst at the same time telling him to move.

Most importantly do not become pinned into a corner. The situation where a horse is threatening and there is no escape is very dangerous and nerve wracking.

Work slowly and quietly around the horse. Avoid any loud noises or sudden movements.

Be aware all the time of the body language of the horse. Ears flat back does not always mean that he will bite or kick but it is a warning and it does certainly show that the horse is not happy.

General Principles of Yard Work

Physical Fitness

Stable work is strenuous, mucking out, grooming, carrying heavy buckets, bales or feed bags. All these jobs need physical fitness, particularly in the area of the back. In the examination one of the group will be asked to describe the method of lifting a straw bale or feed bag. The examiner may even request that candidates do this then and there. A bale of straw, hay or a feed bag will be made available.

Method

Keeping the back straight, bend the knees and go down to the bale. Then lift it up by straightening the legs; this takes quite a bit of thigh strength. Gently swing the bag or bale over the shoulder and carry on the back.

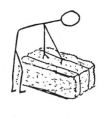

Incorrect   Painful

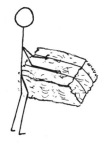

Correct   Successful

It is safer and easier to carry a heavy weight by wheelbarrow or with the assistance of another person.

When carrying water by bucket always have two buckets, one in each hand for balance. One bucket carried on its own will cause an overload on one side and twist the body. Any damage to muscles or bones will not only affect your work but also your riding.

Back ache, slipped discs, pulled or strained muscles are a constant hazard in stable work. It may seem unimportant to lift heavy weights correctly but it can save days, weeks or months of damage and pain to the back.

Clothing

Wearing the right clothes for the job is essential for safety. Strong footwear for stable work; boots or muckers that can withstand wet, muddy conditions and will protect the feet and toes from crushing or blows. Depending on the weather, shirts, jumpers or jackets properly fastened and trousers or jodhpurs that will not interfere with work or become entangled with stable tools and equipment. Long hair should be tied back away from the face. Scarves or caps are suitable as long as they are not likely to flap around or fly off at an inconvenient moment. Ideally jewellery should not be worn at all; even rings can catch up in tack or clothing causing injuries. Most people would wish to retain their wedding ring and providing this fits well and is not loose there is a minimum risk of injury. Large earrings should never be worn. These can easily become entangled and ripped off, causing damage to the ear and face.

Hats and gloves should be worn at specific times; when dealing with vicious, nervous and young horses or when leading. Though gloves should not be worn when grooming; the handler needs to be able to feel for any injuries, heat or swellings on the horse.

Although it is almost impossible to keep squeaky clean whilst doing stable work, smartness in an owner/rider or handler creates a good impression and it generally follows that a smart person means a smart and well-cared for horse.

Stable Equipment

It is essential that all stable tools are cared for, cleaned and stored correctly. Stable equipment includes shaving forks, pitch forks, brooms, skips, wheel barrows, water buckets, feed buckets, haynets, mucking out sacks, shovels or spades, mangers and feed trolleys.

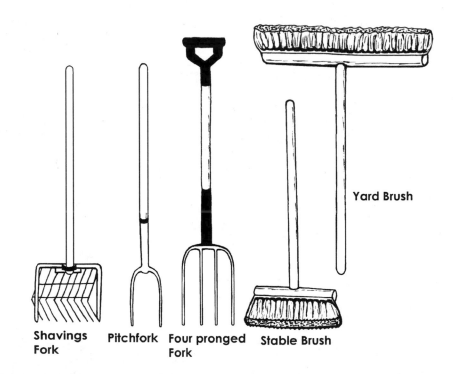

Shavings Fork   Pitchfork   Four pronged Fork   Stable Brush   Yard Brush

Working around horses is dangerous enough without the added problem of misuse and neglect of stable equipment. Keeping equipment clean and in good order is essential. It will last longer, be easier to use and save time. Cleanliness and hygiene will also minimize the risk of infection or disease being transmitted around the yard.

Everything should be tidied away after use. This is not merely for the tidiness of the yard or because equipment is expensive, but also to avoid injury to both workers and horses. Many injuries caused by carelessness result in stitches, broken bones or worse. A rusty or dirty pitchfork, for instance, left lying around may result in a puncture wound which can cause tetanus (lock jaw).

Care must be taken with regard to electrical equipment such as clippers or grooming machines. These must always be used by a competent person, in a safe manner, cleaned and stored properly after use.

It is essential that everyone involved in horse care is taught to use all stable equipment carefully and correctly.

Exam Tip

During the practical session the examiners will not only be assessing the tasks performed by the candidates, but will also observe each individual's behaviour around the horses.

They will be watching how you approach a strange animal, how you enter a box, pick up a horse's foot, treat the horse whilst tacking up or grooming.

Always make sure that the horse is properly secured before handling him. Talk to him. It is all too easy to focus all the attention on the examiner or the job in hand and totally ignore the horse. Providing you do not interrupt the examiner or appear inattentive it is a good idea, especially when holding the horse, to give him an occasional pat or talk to him.

There may be a skip, a fork and a shovel placed outside each exam box. These are there for the purpose of removing any droppings that the horse may pass during the session. If there is time at the end of a discussion or question period, the droppings may be removed. If you do wish to do this, make sure that the horse is adequately restrained first.

C H A P T E R   4
Psychology

Those herds of horses as portrayed in Westerns roaming the plains and occasionally stampeding off into the distance, may seem far removed from the docile animal living its life in a box, whose day consists of eating, working and occasionally grazing in the paddock. Despite how domesticated the horse may now seem, it is still an animal whose behaviour and actions are based on instincts inherited from untamed ancestors.

When working with horses it is necessary to understand their psychology, to know the reactions caused by certain stimuli, to be aware of body language and warning sounds. The most important reason is safety, to avoid danger or injury. This is also essential for the mental and physical health of the horse, to know when the horse is unhappy or ill and to discover the reason for this.

Natural Lifestyle

There are very few herds of wild horses or ponies living free these days and those that do survive, are mostly in remote regions of the world. In their natural habitat horses roam the grasslands, pastures, hills and moorlands in search of food and water. They live in herds for safety and are protected by the dominant stallion who warns the herd of approaching danger.

In the wild a horse's reflexes need to be sharp and quick to survive. A young foal must have the ability to move soon after birth, staying with the herd if it stampedes from danger. Only when cornered will a horse fight and defend itself by kicking, rearing or biting. Sharp hearing, good peripheral vision and speed are necessary for survival in the wild.

Many of the characteristics and instincts derived from the wild are still prevalent in the domesticated animal today. We need to know what these are if we are to understand why the horse reacts the way he does.

Characteristics

The horse has certain qualities or traits that are part of its nature. It behaves and lives in a specific way which makes it different from many other animals.

Herd animal

The horse needs the company of its own kind or in some cases the presence of another animal.

The herd lifestyle is a protective device derived from prehistoric times when horses were hunted and killed by other animals. There is safety in numbers; a chance of escaping attack by predators. The odds are greater for survival in a crowd.

At times horses seem to be constantly fighting, bickering, squealing and kicking each other but they are gregarious and become fretful if left alone. This is often apparent in the field when the horse will show stress by running along a fence, whinnying or even jumping the obstacle to be near the others. Some horses are quite content to be with other animals such as sheep or cows, but few are happy on their own.

This herd characteristic can also cause problems for novice riders and those on young and poorly trained horses. The horse may be reluctant, or the rider not competent enough, to make the horse leave the group or stable yard. This is commonly called 'napping'.

On the other hand this characteristic can be used to a rider's advantage; an older, more experienced horse may lead a younger, reluctant novice over a jump.

Nomadic

In the natural state the herd wanders in search of food, grazing constantly on vegetation and moving from pasture to pasture. Most horses are now enclosed within fields but even here the nomadic instinct is still apparent. The horses will move forwards slowly eating the grass and at times move off to another patch. Interestingly though, horses have a homing instinct that is strong in the modern, domesticated animal. Often a horse which is bolting with or without its rider will make for home or, if the rider is lost, the horse will find its way back to the stable. They all tend to increase their pace towards the direction of home.

Grazing

The horse is a vegetarian eating grass, herbs, shrubs and leaves. He eats small amounts constantly, grazing for 16-20 hours per day and resting only for short periods. This is called 'trickle feeding'. The domesticated horse, therefore, has a totally alien lifestyle being fed unnatural foods at specified times.

Defensive Mechanisms

Most of their reactions reflect the fact that horses are the victims of predators. Their defence is based on either **flight or fight**. The first reaction is to flee, however if cornered, a horse will fight either by biting, kicking, bucking, barging or rearing ~ a foreleg can kick just as well as a hind.

Curiosity

The horse has a tremendous amount of curiosity; often wandering over to investigate something unusual. This trait can be used to catch an awkward horse in the field. My horse, if he is playing hard to get, cannot bear me standing a little way from him fiddling with something, especially if I turn my back to him. Then he will generally walk right up to me and put his head over my shoulder.

Dominant Animal

The horse is certainly not a democrat. But then, in the wild, deciding to escape from a pack of wolves does not allow much time for discussion! Much more practical to have one dominant male, a stallion, and follow his lead. He cares for the herd sensing danger and giving warning, searching out food and drink. In many ways the human has taken over this role for the domesticated animal.

In the domestic herd there is one dominant male or female and a pecking order for the rest. The pecking order of seniority depends on assertiveness and strength.

Imitators

Horses tend to imitate others and it is possible that they pick up bad habits this way, such as weaving or crib-biting.

Good memory

A horse has an excellent memory particularly for pain. If he has been badly treated at some point in his life then, in a similar situation, he will tend to be awkward in future. It is therefore important that the horse is handled correctly from an early age.

As an aid to memory and recall, keywords have been included in the text to make learning easier.

Key Words to Characteristics

- ❖ Herd
- ❖ Nomadic
- ❖ Flight or fight
- ❖ Grazers
- ❖ Curiosity
- ❖ Pecking order
- ❖ Imitators
- ❖ Memory

Instincts

Horses have very strong instinctive behaviour. Instincts are present in an animal from birth; they are emotional responses to situations or influences. In a horse these emotions are shown by physical indications such as body language and noises.

Fear

A horse that is frightened in the open will generally bolt. He may spin round quickly then flee. Sometimes in a field the horse will run from the object of fear but then turn to face the potential enemy. If the threat is no longer apparent, the horse may tentatively approach the object, head lowered, sniffing or blowing but still tensed and ready to run.

On a ride a sudden movement or noise may make the horse jump quickly to the side away from the threat. If the danger persists he may turn quickly and bolt.

In a stable he will retreat to the farthest point away from the object of fear. His head will be held high facing towards the danger, eyes wide and staring, nostrils dilated and blowing, ears pricked and mobile to pick up sound. The body will be side on to the threat, held taut, rise and grow in height, muscles tight and tense.

Nervousness

The head will be held high with eyes wide and alert, nostrils flared, blowing or snorting, ears mobile, pricked and listening. The body will rise and tense, preparing for flight. The horse may quiver, shake or start to sweat. His rate of breathing may increase. He may pass droppings frequently.

Anger

An angry horse holds his head slightly lowered, ears back, laid flat on the neck, eyes mean looking and narrowed, lips curled, teeth bared. He will show an aggressive posture and hindquarters may swing round. He may try to bite or kick.

Pain

The horse will run from external pain, bolting. When cornered his head may be raised and eyes narrowed, he will rear, kick or bite. The important aspect of pain is that the horse remembers it for a long time.

If the rider is causing the pain the horse will not only bolt but try and throw the rider off either by rearing or bucking. Bucking, in some cases, is a defence against a threat from the rear. This would originally have been an attack by wolves or other predators jumping on the horse's back. Bucking can also be a sign of enjoyment and excitement.

Contentment

The horse will appear relaxed and calm, his body soft, his coat shining. His ears will be mobile moving gently to sound.

Unhappiness

He will appear introspective, dull, lifeless, lethargic, angry or antagonistic. His head will be held down, eyes dull, ears floppy, body drooping and tired looking, the coat rough. Sometimes horses develop bad habits such as aggressive behaviour or stable vices.

Interest

The neck will be arched, nostrils sniffing, ears mobile, body alert but relaxed. The eyes are bright and the muzzle pointed forward, searching.

Excitement

Here the head is held high, nostrils flared and sniffing, breathing possibly quickened, ears pricked and eyes bright. The horse will be prancing around possibly bucking; body alert, tail held erect. He may sweat.

Naughty

The ears will be held back but not flat. The eyes will look shifty and narrowed, watching and mean. The nostrils will contract and tighten. The horse may try to cow kick, or lift a back leg.

Playful

The horse may paw the ground with a front foot. He will move quickly, running with short steps then turning and bucking. Play is seen mostly in foals but all horses play sometimes.

Attentive

The ears are pricked and mobile, eyes bright and alert. The body is relaxed but held ready.

Fighting for Dominance

The head may either be held down with neck outstretched or held up with neck arched. The teeth may be bared, lips curled; ears laid flat back; the eyes small and mean. The body is stretched out and menacing. Sometimes the horse will paw the ground with a foreleg, or swing round the hindquarters ready for kicking.

Verbal Sounds

The verbal sounds a horse makes can be a clear indication of emotion or of an impending action.

Neigh	Normally a call to other horses or a method of attracting attention. Often heard when a mare is separated from her foal.
Whinny	A high pitched sound associated with excitement and tension.
Nicker	A non-aggressive call to a nearby horse, recognition of a person or anticipation of pleasure (usually food).
Snort	Indicates excitement, playfulness or annoyance. It can also be used as one of the first signs of fear or for expelling dust from the nostrils.
Scream	Expresses intense anger, aggression, fear and pain.
Blow	Used when scenting territory or smelling horse dung
Bellow	A sound of authority, often used by stallions when challenged.
Squeal	Comes from a mare in season or excited foals at play. A mare may use it to scold a foal
Sigh	Can mean contentment or boredom.

When working or training with horses for a length of time, grooms, riders and handlers become aware of the sounds that horses make, often relating to it as a language. For instance hearing a squeal from within a field, the handler will be almost certain there is a fight going on.

One of the most rewarding sounds is to hear my horse nicker to me first thing in the morning. I always imagine he is saying 'Hello Mum', though in reality he is probably anticipating his breakfast!

Exam Tip

The Stage I examination covers a great deal of horse psychology with examiners asking about equine behaviour, body language, characteristics and instincts. You may be asked to explain the horse's natural lifestyle and the differences apparent in the domesticated animal. You may have to describe the horse's reaction in certain situations; when he is frightened in the stable or on a ride, how a new horse to the yard would show that he is nervous. Practise explaining how a horse shows anger, pain or aggression.

The examiners may ask you to explain why some horses and ponies become difficult to catch, how an awkward horse might be caught and how his behaviour could be improved in future. You will need to know how a horse reacts when turned out in a field with other strange horses, how the herd sorts out the pecking order and how you could recognize the 'boss'. You may have to describe how horses act in a field normally and what you would expect from a pony being turned out to grass for the first time in weeks. The chapter on Grassland Management gives more information on the behaviour of horses and ponies in the field.

Each group of candidates may be requested to list some of the instincts of the horse and to explain what emotions can be detected from the position of the horse's ears or tail. You will need to observe the horse in all situations in the stable and in the field. Watch the horse's body language and how he reacts to other horses within the yard.

Working with horses develops an awareness of their body language and reactions, so that you almost instinctively know how they will act in certain situations. However being able to describe this to an examiner who throws a situation at you can be very difficult. You will need to practise imagining situations and describing how the horse will react and the signals given by his body language.

C H A P T E R   5

Physiology

This section deals with the physical aspect of the horse, the main external areas, points, colours and markings. It is in itself a fascinating subject but it also develops understanding of how the horse's system functions.

External Areas

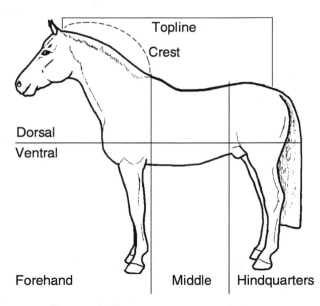

Figure 18: The external areas of the horse.

Forehand	From head to withers including the forelegs.
Middle	The barrel of the horse including the back and belly.
Hindquarters	From the loins including hind legs and tail.
Topline	The top area from the poll to the dock including the crest.
Crest	Top portion of the neck from the poll to the withers.
Dorsal section	The upper half of the body from just above the legs.
Ventral section	The lower half of the horse.

Points   When referred to with regard to colouring are; the tips of the ears, mane, tail and the legs from the hoof to just above the knees and hocks. e.g. a bay is brown with black points.

(These should not be confused with Points of the Horse.)

Figure 19: Pony with Black Points.

Points   When referring to external areas are the names given to specific locations on the horse's body. These are often used to judge the quality or standard of a horse.

Points of a Horse

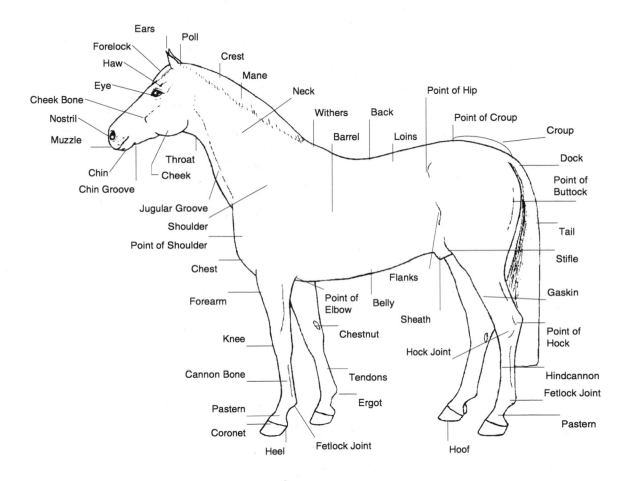

The points of the horse are not only a convenient method of distinguishing external areas, they are also necessary for the further study of the internal anatomy.

Classification

Difference between a horse and a pony

A horse or pony is basically determined by size, though build and movement can also be taken into consideration. Generally speaking any animal 14.2 hands and under is classed as a pony, above 14.2 h.h. may be described as a horse.

A horse or pony is measured with a measuring stick. The animal must be stood on level ground and the measurement is then taken to the highest point of the wither. The size is calculated in hands, one hand equals 4 inches. Shoes can account for approximately a quarter of an inch.

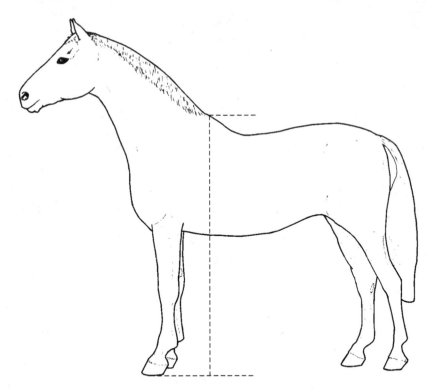

Figure 20: Measuring the height of a horse.

Accurate measurement of height is important when selling or buying a horse, for competitions or showing classes which are restricted to height and for a guide when buying tack or clothing.

Gender

A female horse or pony is a **filly** up to the age of four when she becomes a **mare.**

A **colt** is a male horse or pony under the age of four.

A **gelding** is a castrated male horse or pony. Castration is usually performed when the horse or pony is around a year old. Some heavy breeds are often left until three or four.

If the horse remains **'entire',** that is, not castrated, the colt becomes a **stallion.** Most male horses if not used for breeding are gelded.

Age

Age, unless specifically known, is determined mainly by the teeth. Other signs of age are the haw, the hollow above the eye which tends to deepen with age, and the general angularity of the shape of the horse or pony. The bony areas appear more prominent with age.

Breeds

Many horses and ponies are descended from pure strains or breeds. For an animal to be classed as a breed its ancestry must be pure, e.g. Welsh Mountain, New Forest, Arab. Most pure bred horses and ponies are registered and have papers as proof of their ancestry. Most breeds have distinguishing features in height, colour, markings and temperament.

Horses or ponies of mixed blood are generally classed in 'types'. Their ancestry may not be known or proved but they exhibit the characteristics of a breed or type; for example, a middleweight hunter, a New Forest type.

Many horses are referred to as either hot, warm or cold-blooded, although literally speaking all are warmblooded mammals. Hot-bloods are usually breeds originating in the East such as Arabs or Barbs. Cold-bloodeds include heavy work horses such as Clydesdales. Warm-bloods are a mixture of the two and include Danish and Dutch Warm-bloods.

Hot-blooded horses are usually more highly strung and may be temperamental whereas cold-blooded horses are generally quieter and steadier.

Native Breeds

There are nine Mountain and Moorland breeds which originate naturally within the United Kingdom and Eire. All nine breeds however are extremely hardy having survived centuries of an environment that can be severe, especially in winter.

The nine native breeds indigenous to the British Isles are:

* Shetland

* Highland

* Fell

* Dale

* Welsh

* New Forest

* Exmoor

* Dartmoor

* Connemara

Figure 21: Native breeds of the British Isles.

Other British breeds include the Thoroughbred, (descended from three Arab stallions brought to Britain during the 17th/18th centuries), the Anglo-Arab and the British Warm-blood which is a relatively new strain. There is also the Shire, Clydesdale, Suffolk Punch, Cleveland Bay, Irish Draught and the Hackney.

Colours

The colour of a horse is created by skin pigment, hair colour and markings on the body. Most breeds have distinguishing colours derived from their environment or selective breeding. In some cases in the Show world a horse of a particular breed must have the 'correct' colour. Colours and markings are also an important part of the identification process, when it is imperative that they are described accurately. These are used on the horse's passport or identity card.

Colour is an important consideration when buying a horse as it often indicates temperament and possible future care needed. A good strong colour often signifies hardiness. White markings can mean that the skin in those areas is sensitive, for instance horses with white markings around the heels may be more prone to mud fever. Chestnut mares are often expected to have a fiery or awkward nature. Pure greys can be difficult to keep clean and are more prone to skin cancer in old age.

Black   True black is very rare. An apparent black horse may be very dark brown or bay. To check this look at the flank or under the belly for any slight variation in shading.

Brown   This colour must cover most of the body and there should be no black points.

Bay   Brown with black points - mane, tips of ears, tail and legs are black. Bays can vary from a bright bay, light in colour to a dark, mahogany bay.

Chestnut   A reddish colour that can vary from a bright 'tomato soup' shade to a dark 'liver' chestnut. A chestnut can also have a **flaxen** mane and tail - the mane and tail are light coloured, either silver or cream.

Grey   Often mistakenly called white, **pure greys** usually have a mixture of white hairs on a dark skin. A close look by ruffling the hair will show the colour of the skin underneath.

A **dappled grey** has circles of darker hair.

The unfortunately named **flea-bitten grey** has little tufts of dark hair, usually brown, all over the body.

An **iron grey** is very dark, sometimes almost black in appearance.

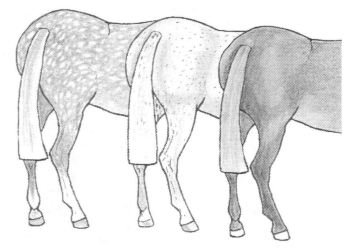

Figure 22: Dapple, Flea-bitten & Iron grey.

Albino   This is rare and occurs where the skin has no pigmentation. The appearance is pinkish-white all over with pink eyes and muzzle. This colouring produces the only true 'white' horses or ponies.

Palomino   This is a golden colour varying from very light to a rich, dark shade with white mane and tail.

Cream   A pale, cream colour on a pink skin. The mane and tail are often silver. Sometimes creams have blue or 'wall' eyes.

Piebald   A horse with two colours, black and white in irregular patches.

Skewbald   Similar to the piebald except the patches are brown and white.

Odd-colour Consists of more than two colours, usually black, brown and white.

Spotted   Horses classed as spotteds have a colour that consists of patterns of spots usually on roan or white. The most famous spotted horse of all, the **Appaloosa,** is a breed that originated in North America, though not all spotted horses are appaloosas.

There are five basic patterns:

Leopard-spotted has spots of any colour on a light coat.

Blanket-spotted has spots on the back and hind-quarters only.

'Snowflake' and **'Frosted'** have white spots on a dark coat.

Marble is a mottled colour.

Figure 23: Leopard, Blanket, Snowflake, Frosted & Marble Spotted.

Roan	There are three main types of roan.

A **blue roan** has a mixture of black-brown and white hair that produces a bluish appearance, a black mane, tail and legs.

A **strawberry roan** is a mixture of chestnut and white hair.

A **bay roan** is brown hair with white.

Dun	A **dark or mouse dun** is, as the name suggests, the colour of a mouse.

A **silver dun** appears silvery.

A **yellow dun** is a light lemon colour.

A **golden dun** is a rich gold.

Duns do vary from very light to dark but most have **black points**, a **list or dorsal stripe** and **zebra markings** on the legs. Native and ancient breeds usually have a dun colour, such as the Highland.

Eye Colouring

Most horse's eyes are brown but occasionally there will be different colours such as yellow or blue. These are usually associated with colouring or face markings.

Wall Eye is where one or both eyes are either completely blue or bluish.

Markings

All horses have markings whether caused by a different colour, for instance on the legs and face, or by the hair lying in a different direction from the rest of the coat. These are important as they identify the horse by being individual distinguishing marks and may sometimes indicate the nature of a horse or give clues to any weaknesses that may occur. They can also be evidence of previous treatment, for instance white markings on the saddle area or on the legs can indicate past injuries.

White Marks

Natural white markings usually occur on the head or limbs. A horse that has no white markings at all is called whole-coloured.

Head Markings

Feint

A small touch of white usually in the middle of the forehead.

Star

A larger white mark on the forehead.

Stripe

A narrow strip of white down the face usually starting from the forehead and finishing around the nostrils.

Blaze

A broad strip extending usually from the forehead to the nostrils.

White face

A white marking that covers most of the face, forehead, nostrils and mouth.

Snip

A small white marking between the nostrils.

White muzzle

White on the mouth and around nostrils.

White lip

White around the mouth, either upper or lower lip or both.

Leg markings

Areas of white hair on the legs, from the fetlock down, are named after the portions covered;

*   A white **coronet, heel, pastern** and **fetlock.**

Areas of white above the fetlock are described as follows:

*   A **sock** is a white marking from hoof to just above the fetlock.

*   A **stocking** is white from the hoof to below the hock or knee.

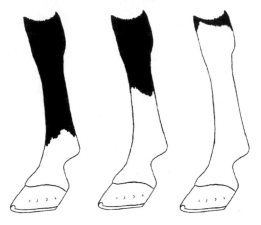

*   A **white leg** is white beyond the knee or hock.

Ermine marks

These occur in areas of white hair and appear as black spots on the white rather like the pattern of an ermine fur. Usually evident on the legs around the coronet or pastern. Can be very small, not always clearly visible.

Further Markings

As well as the normal markings on legs and head, there are other variations of colour or lie of coat which every horse and pony exhibits. Some are so small or hidden that a close inspection is required to find them.

Zebra markings

As the name suggests these are markings arranged in a pattern of black zebra stripes. They occur usually on the back of both fore and hind legs and are a characteristic of some breeds such as the Highland. On light coloured horses and ponies these markings are quite distinctive whereas on a naturally darker animal the stripes are more difficult to see.

List or dorsal line

This is a black stripe stretching from the base of the mane to the top of the tail all along the back bone. Again this is a characteristic of certain breeds, as in the Highland and Norwegian Fjord.

Mixed or bordered

On coloured horses, piebald, skewbald or odd-coloured the patches of darker colour can sometimes have a border of a different colour.

Flecked and ticked markings

On darker coloured animals flecked markings are apparent as white patches of hair, ticked markings show up as small, thin stripes. These can either be all over the animal or cover barrel, belly and flank only.

Liver and strawberry mark

These show up as dark patches on a lighter coat. Liver marks usually occur on chestnuts and strawberry marks on greys.

Toad Eye

This appears as a lighter shading surrounding the eyes.

Mealy Muzzle

Where the shading of the muzzle is lighter or cream in colour. The mealy muzzle and toad eye are characteristics of certain breeds such as the Exmoor pony.

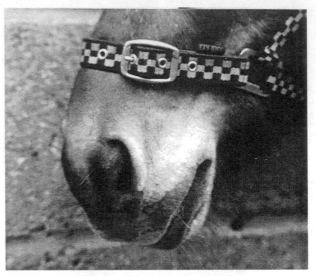

Figure 24: A mealy muzzle.

Flesh marks

These are normally found on light coloured horses or those with a white face or light coloured muzzle. Around the muzzle the skin is pink where the pigment is absent. Darker areas of skin show up in patches.

Hair Markings

Whorl

The hair lies in a different direction to the coat usually occurring on the forehead, neck, chest and flanks. Whorls can vary in size and are usually arranged in circles or lines. They are individual to each horse and are an excellent means of identification.

Injury marks

These are apparent particularly on darker coloured horses where the hair has grown white over an old injury. They are particularly evident around the saddle and girth areas or on the legs around the site of wounds or damage.

Prophet, miller's or devil's thumbprint

Small thumb sized indentations in the muscles, usually on the neck and shoulder areas.

Horn

Chestnuts

The horny growths, one on the inside of all four legs, have characteristics which are unique to each horse. They are reputed to be as individual as fingerprints and are used as a form of identification. On the foreleg chestnuts are just above the knee and on the hind legs just below the hock.

Hoof colours

Again markings on the hooves are supposed to be unique to each horse and many owners take photographs of their horse's hooves for identification. Hooves are usually dark, markings here include white stripes or patches, normally associated with white leg markings. Occasionally horses have a white hoof.

Artificial Marks

Many owners wish to identify their animals more positively and have various markings put on parts of the body.

Freeze marking

A method of identification marking. A listed number is applied by extreme cold turning the hair white. In the case of greys the marking turns pink. This remains on the horse as a permanent feature for life. A national register is kept of all freeze-marked horses and this acts as a deterrent to thieves.

Figure 25: Freeze Mark.

Note: Injury marks on withers caused by an ill fitting saddle in the past.

A Brand

This is a scar on the skin made by a hot iron. Many countries practise this method and it is also used specifically for various breeds of horse.

Lip and Ear Tattoo

As the name implies numbers are tattooed into the skin usually on the ear or under the top lip.

Hoof brand

The farrier brands letters or numbers, sometimes a postcode, onto the hoof wall. This has the disadvantage of eventually growing out.

Tail trims

A section of the horses tail is cut. Used particularly to identify native wild breeds. Again, this type of identification will eventually grow out.

Exam Tip

For the session on anatomy each candidate will be required to name several points of the horse usually showing their relative position. As this is a group session you could be asked to start from anywhere on the horse. For instance, if you are fourth or fifth in the group you may be required to name the points on the hindquarters or legs. When studying for the exam, try repeating the points starting from different areas of the horse's body.

During this session also candidates will be asked to examine a horse briefly and describe its colour and markings. A general discussion will follow about further colours, natural or artificial markings and distinguishing features. Practise looking at horses closely and identifying colours and markings.

C H A P T E R   6
Health

For all horse owners, or those who have horses in their charge, it is essential to be able to recognize when a horse is suffering from ill health. Often the signs are not glaringly evident and may simply be a slight change in behaviour. Recognition is vital if diagnosis and treatment are to be effective.

The first duty in the daily routine is to check that the horse is in good health. For a stabled horse a quick observation will usually be sufficient to notice if anything is radically wrong. In the case of field kept animals a check can be made either from the gate or from within the field if the horses are out of sight.

Closer inspections must be done later in the day. Horses and ponies in whatever environment must be thoroughly checked at least once a day. This is particularly essential for those living out at grass permanently.

Good Health

The basic sign that the horse is in good health is that he is **behaving normally**, acting in his usual manner. If he has his head out over the door first thing in the morning, nickering and holding his head high, this is a good sign that he is well.

He may, on the other hand, be the sort of horse who normally stands in the box looking dozy and quiet, perhaps with one hind leg resting. In this case if he became restless in the box looking agitated then it would be obvious that something was wrong.

It is therefore, important to **'know your horse'**, be aware of his normal mannerisms and be alert for anything that is unusual in his behaviour. 'Know your horse' is an excellent cliché to remember. (The horse world is full of clichés which, being generally founded on centuries of experience and knowledge, are a good guideline to Horse Care.)

Initial Signs

In the Stable

- The horse is **bright** and **alert** with **ears pricked, moving to sound**.

- He is **interested** in his surroundings. Even if he is standing at the back of his box he should look round and come over to the door should his handler call.

- His **coat** is **dry** and **glossy, lying smoothly** over the **bones** and **muscles**.

- His **eyes** and **nostrils** should be **clean**.

- He is **breathing regularly**.

- He is **standing square** on **all four legs**. (A hind leg is often rested. However, should the horse always rest the same hind and not wish to use it properly when exercising; it would be a warning note.)

The Bed

- Should be fairly **neat.**

- The **number of dung piles is correct** and of the **right consistency** for his diet. (Horses can pass about eight to ten piles of dung a day. Usually in the morning there will be about four to five piles.)

His Food

- Should **certainly be eaten** and though some can be fussy eaters, a horse should never miss more than one feed. He should also have **drunk some water**.

All this can be noticed from the first check in the morning or when the horse is being watered and fed.

In the field.

The normal behaviour of the horse or pony kept permanently at pasture depends on the **time of the year**.

During the spring, summer and early autumn:

- The horse should be **with the herd** or a little way apart.

- He should be **grazing** or standing near the others perhaps **nuzzling necks or flicking each other with tails**.

- Some may lie down for a while near the herd but all should look **relaxed** and **at ease**.

On winter mornings:

- The **herd** will be gathered by the gate, or wherever the food is brought in to the field.

- They may **stand close together** for warmth, or be **tentatively grazing** at patches of grass.

- All should look **bright** and **alert, anticipating food.**

Thorough Check

A good time to do this is when grooming or brushing down before exercise.

- The **coat** should **feel soft, shiny and smooth**.

- The limbs should be **cool** and **free of swellings, lumps, wounds and sores**. This check is made by running the hand down each leg.

- When the feet are cleaned they can be checked. The **hooves** should be **cool,** and the foot underneath **free of any bruising, discoloration of sole or horn, wounds or stones.**

- The horse should be a **normal warm temperature**, not sweating unduly, shivering or trembling. Feeling the base of the ears is a good way of determining temperature. They should be warm, not hot or cold.

- The horse's **eyes** should be **clear, free of discharge**.

- His **nostrils** should be **clean and dry**.

- The **membranes** of the **eyes, gums and nostrils** can also be inspected; these should be **salmon pink** in colour. If they are white, red, bluish or purple, this can be a sign of trouble.

- The horse's **general demeanour** should be **alert** but **relaxed, interested** but **not agitated**.

- He should **stand on all four feet evenly** when asked to do so.

Basic Rules To Keep A Horse Healthy:

- ★ Visit the horse every day checking for good health.
- ★ Make sure that all necessary inoculations are given on time.
- ★ Worm regularly.
- ★ Feed correctly.
- ★ Make sure that clean water is available constantly.
- ★ Maintain hygiene and cleanliness in the stable and with clothing.
- ★ Groom daily.
- ★ Maintain shoeing correctly and regularly.
- ★ Make sure the horse is warm enough and well rugged up in winter.

★   Check all fields and pasture daily.

★   Avoid contact with horses that have infectious or contagious diseases.

★   Exercise horse properly.

Ill Health

In many cases it is obvious that the horse is ill but just as frequently the signs are extremely small and subtle. **Any deviation from normal behaviour must be closely monitored.** This may not signify physical ill health but generally if a horse behaves abnormally then something is wrong.

Initial Signs

❖   If the horse is standing at the back of the box looking **lethargic and droopy,** this could signify that he is not in good health especially if he will not turn round when called.

❖   He may be **sweating or show visible dried sweat marks.**

❖   He may be **trembling** or **shivering.**

❖   His whole body may be **'tucked up'** with his back rounded and his **tail held tight** against his hindquarters.

❖   He may be **kicking at his flank** or trying to **bite his sides**.

❖   His **feed or hay may remain uneaten** or **water untouched.**

❖   If he is wearing a **rug** this may be **torn or askew.**

On a Closer Inspection

❖   His **eyes** may be **dull**.

❖   **Ears immobile** and **drooping**.

❖   There may be **discharge** from **eyes** and **nostrils** or evidence of such on the floor or door.

❖   His **coat** may be **dull and 'stary'**, that is instead of lying flat the hair sticks out from the body.

❖   His **breathing** could be **irregular** or he may be **wheezing, coughing** or **sneezing.**

- ❖ It may be obvious that he has had a **disturbed night**; the **bedding** may be **tossed** around or heaped in the middle of the box. There may be signs that the **walls, floor** or **door** have been **kicked**.

- ❖ There may be **no dung** or what there is may be **too soft or too hard**. There could be signs of **diarrhoea** down his hind legs (known as **scouring**).

- ❖ He may be **pointing a foot**; only the toe of the foreleg touches the ground and the heel is raised.

- ❖ His **legs** may look **swollen and painful.**

- ❖ His **hooves** may feel **hot** to touch.

Figure 26: Pointing a Foot.

In the Field

- ❖ Here the horse may be standing at the gate looking **sorry for himself**.

- ❖ He may stand **apart from the herd** looking **droopy** and **dishevelled**.

- ❖ He would appear **uninterested in food**.

- ❖ He may be **lying down** for long periods, have difficulty rising or be **rolling** constantly.

- ❖ He may be **pointing or keeping the weight off the fore feet**, leaning back on his hind legs.

- ❖ He may be **shivering and trembling**.

- ❖ He may even be **lame,** so it is important to see the horse move, if only in walk.

Report

When any sign of ill health appears it is vital that a report is made to senior staff or someone in control. It is far better to be safe than sorry, that care is taken immediately before the horse becomes seriously ill. Even a matter of an hour or so could make a difference.

Also, it is the groom's responsibility that the horse is properly cared for and monitored. Any delay in reporting abnormal or worrying behaviour, which then leads to ill health, will reflect back on the groom.

Daily Routines

A routine is a regular method of procedure. There are two main reasons why such a method is important for Horse Care; the welfare of the horse and the efficient running of the yard.

1. **'Horses thrive on routine'** another equestrian cliché that is completely true. For physical and mental reasons horses need a routine.

   Physically   The horse needs to be fed little and often. Having a small stomach, (roughly the size of a rugby ball with a capacity of 4 - 6 lb.), he cannot eat large amounts at one meal. Food can also take 2 to 4 hours to pass through the stomach leaving a horse feeling hungry about 5 hours after being fed. To follow as closely as possible his natural feeding habits and to keep his digestive system working properly, the horse must be fed small amounts at regular intervals.

   Mentally   Horses become nervy and apprehensive when faced with constant change. Just the simple act of always picking out the feet in a routine way helps to keep the horse in a happy frame of mind. Horses seem to have an in-built clock, especially for feed times, and will soon become used to a routine of feeding, grooming, exercising and pasture time. If for any reason these times are changed they can become excited or anxious.

2. The efficient running of a yard and the organisation of horse care depends on a routine of work. Jobs organised for the same time every day are easier to complete. The human mind works better if programmed to a routine timetable.

Daily routines will necessarily be different for each stable and depend upon several factors:

- Type of yard and therefore the work the horses are doing.
- Time of year.
- Availability of workers.
- Number of horses.
- Visits by Vets or Farrier.

The only variables should be in cases of competitions, shows, outings and different types of work to avoid the horse becoming stale.

The basic elements of a routine are; that the horses are **watered** and **fed regularly**, **exercised**, **groomed**, **mucked out** and allowed **rest** or **pasture time**, that **tack is cleaned** and the **stable yard tidied**.

To create a practical timetable for a yard, a chart is worked out for the necessary jobs, those that must be accomplished at certain times of the day. Other tasks can be fitted in when convenient.

A sample routine

07.30	Check horse. Clean out water bucket and refill. Give hay net and morning feed. **Have breakfast**.
09.00	Tie horse up safely preferably with a haynet. Muck out stable. Clean yard around stable. Give horse a brush down and pick out his feet.
10.00	Tack up and exercise.
11.30	Untack after exercise and groom thoroughly. Rug up if necessary.
12.30	Refill water bucket. Give a small feed.
13.00	Put on New Zealand if necessary and turn horse out into field. Skip out stable. **Lunch**.
14.30	Clean and check tack, once a week thoroughly. Wash numnah and boots for next day. Dry in airing cupboard.
16.00	Bring horse in from grass. Give small haynet. Brush down and pick out feet.
17.00	Tea.
18.00	Skip out and put down night bed. Refill water. Put up haynets.
20.00	Night feed. Refill water. Set Fair for night.

This routine applies to one horse - in a busy yard where there are a number of working pupils and the horses are worked regularly during the day, the routine will vary.

Exam Tip

For the session on health, individuals within the group will be asked to describe the signs of good and ill health and why an immediate report is vital. At this stage candidates do not need to know the causes or treatment of illnesses but simply how to recognize when a horse or pony, in the stable or field, is unwell.

C H A P T E R 7
Headcollars

The horse should always be correctly restrained when anyone is caring or working around him. Grooming, tacking up, putting a rug on, are all safer with the horse tied up with a headcollar and lead rope. There is much less risk of injury.

Types of Headcollars

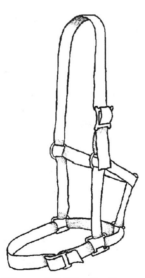

There are varying designs of headcollar but most are made up of a headpiece, a noseband and a throatlash section. Often the noseband and throatlash are connected by a strap.

Figure 27: Headcollar.

Headcollars are usually made from nylon or leather. Nylon is less expensive to buy, available in a variety of colours and easily cleaned by washing in soapy water. Leather is expensive but much smarter in appearance.

Figure 28: Clip on the throatlash.

The fastenings vary too. Most usual is the headcollar that has one fastening on the headpiece, but there are those that also have a clip on the throatlash.

The most useful type is one that features a second clip or buckle on the noseband. This can then be unfastened, when putting the bridle on, and the headcollar placed around the horse's neck easily, without undoing the headpiece buckle.

Figure 29: Buckle on noseband.

Sizes

There are different sizes of headcollar ~ **Pony, Cob, or Full.** The cob size will fit a large pony or even a horse with a small, fine head. However, though headcollars are fairly easy to alter in size, it is not possible for a pony headcollar to fit a heavy hunter!

Halters

The halter is similar to a headcollar but without the throatlash. It is usually made from one piece of rope or webbing. Being less secure than the headcollar, the halter cannot be left on if the horse is untied in the stable nor whilst he is out in the field.

Figure 30: Halter.

Putting on a Headcollar

Approach the horse quietly from the side, walking towards his neck and shoulder. If the horse is likely to be awkward, raising his head or moving around the box, placing the lead rope quietly around his neck first will prevent his misbehaviour.

To prepare the headcollar the buckle on the headpiece should be unfastened. The lead rope may be clipped onto the ring of the headcollar; this prevents fiddling about later and allows a firmer hold when the horse is caught.

Gently slip the nose band on, place the head piece carefully over the head behind the ears and fasten the buckle.

The lead rope is clipped onto the ring underneath the horse's chin. The opening of the clip should face away from the head so that it will not catch the horse's jaw bone.

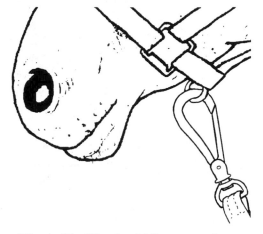

Figure 31: Clip should face away from head.

Fitting

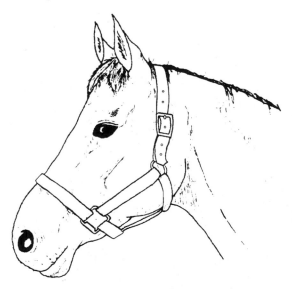

Figure 32: Correctly fitted headcollar.

Once the headcollar has been fastened the fit is checked. The noseband should lie approximately two to three fingers width below the horse's projecting cheek bone. There should be one to two fingers space between it and the horse's face.

The headcollar should fit firmly enough so that it does not slip off should the horse pull back but not so tight as to cause rubbing or pain.

Problems of ill-fitting or dirty headcollars

The fit is important especially if the horse or pony must wear the headcollar in the field. Too loose and the headcollar could become caught up in fences or bushes. Too tight and the result will be a horse with bare patches, which may become sore and infected. Ideally a horse or pony should not need to wear a headcollar when at grass, but there are times when this is unavoidable.

An incorrectly fitted headcollar can cause physical injury and long lasting mental problems. If the headcollar is wrongly fitted or uncomfortable, the horse may try to escape by pulling back. This can cause considerable pain around the poll area, resulting in a horse that is 'head shy' for many years to come.

As with all equipment, clean headcollars and halters are essential to prevent sores, diseases and infections. Most headcollars and lead ropes can be washed either by hand or in the washing machine with unscented soap or non-biological washing powder. Leather headcollars are cleaned in the same way as bridles and saddles, with a sponge, saddle soap and a regular oiling.

Tying Up A Horse

A horse should never be tied directly to a fixed object; a fence, gate, tree, metal ring or trailer. A horse pulling back in a headcollar can panic and injure himself.

The lead rope should always be tied to a piece of string which is attached to the fixed object. Then should the horse pull back, the string breaks under the strain, releasing the pressure on the headcollar and the horse. Many stables use baling twine for this purpose but this is really too strong and does not break easily. String is better or, alternatively, baling twine that has been untwisted.

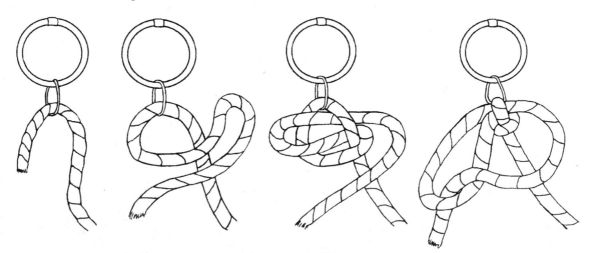

Figure 33: How to tie a quick release knot.

The lead rope is tied to the string with a quick release knot, so that when necessary the horse can be untied quickly.

If dealing with an awkward horse or performing some task on a horse that may make him nervous, the lead rope can be passed through the string without being tied. The end of the rope is held by the handler or an assistant. In the event of the horse pulling back the leadrope can be released easily.

A horse should never be left in a headcollar with the lead rope dangling to the floor. Horses often tread on the rope and pull back immediately, causing damage to themselves and the headcollar.

Tying Up in the Stable

In the stable there are usually metal securing rings to which a loop of string should be attached. There are self releasing rings on the market now which, it is claimed, come out of the wall if the horse pulls back.

The rings should be situated on the side walls of the stable. The horse should never be tied up at the back of the box with his hindquarters facing the door. This is obviously dangerous for anyone entering the box.

Tying Up Outside

When the horse is tied up outside, the surrounding area must be safe.

* The ground must be firm so that the horse is not likely to slip or fall.

* There should be no other horses nearby in case of biting and kicking.

* The horse should not be tied up where vehicles are likely to pass or in a situation where anything else may startle him.

* The horse should be tied where there is sufficient room for him. In a confined space where he cannot move around, the horse may panic and hurt himself.

* He should never be stood near electric cables, hose pipes, taps, sharp objects, water troughs, tree stumps or under low branches.

* The horse should not be left unattended or out of sight for any length of time.

* The leadrope should not be tied too short to restrict the horse's movement, nor too long allowing him to get his leg caught.

How to Stand Horse Up

Holding in a Headcollar

The handler stands on the nearside of the horse facing the front, with the right shoulder by the horse's left shoulder. The lead rope is held near the horse's chin in the right hand; the remainder being held in the left to keep it from trailing on the floor.

For more control the right hand can be reversed so that instead of the fingers uppermost the back of the hand is uppermost and the fingers below. This gives a firmer hold and should the horse try to move off or attempt to barge forwards, he can be restrained by pressing gently with the elbow on the side of his neck. Whips or crops should be held in the left hand.

For Treatment or Inspection

To hold a horse for clipping, the farrier, the vet, or for a prospective buyer, the handler turns around to face the horse, with the left shoulder by the horse's head. The lead rope is now held by the horse's chin in the left hand; the excess and crop being held in the right. In some cases, where a stronger restraint is necessary, the bridle can be used instead of a headcollar.

When holding the horse for treatment or inspection the handler stands on the same side as the inspection is taking place. For instance if the Vet is examining the offside, the handler should also stand to the offside, with the right shoulder next to the horse. The leadrope is held in the right hand near the horse's chin. The handler can now see what the person dealing with the horse is doing and be warned of any action that may startle the horse, ready to calm and control him.

To Stand a Horse Up Correctly

The horse should stand with all four feet level on the ground, the fore feet together and the hind feet together. The horse's head should be raised so that he appears alert. The horse does not look so good with his head drooping. In show circles or for inspection by a prospective buyer, usually the fore feet are together but the near hind foot is farther back than the off hind.

Leading in a Head collar

When leading a horse the handler should always wear gloves and suitable footwear, boots or strong shoes that will not slip. A riding hat is also essential if leading on the public highway or when dealing with a young horse. (In these cases a bridle should replace the headcollar for further security.)

As a rule horses are led from the left or near side, but they should be accustomed to being led from either side.

- Hold the lead rope near the horse's chin in the right hand and the other end in the left. Do not allow the rope to drag on the ground.

- *The lead rope should never be wrapped around the hand.* This is extremely dangerous. In the event of the horse racing off the groom may be dragged along or, at least, end up with considerable physical damage to the hand.

- Facing to the front, stand by the horse's neck just in front of his left shoulder and ask him in a firm voice to 'Walk on'. Taking a small step forwards, encourage the horse to move off and walk beside him so that effectively he is leading.

- *Never get in front of the horse and never, never pull him.* This usually makes him stop, raise his head and in some cases pull back and escape.

- Instead should he stop or refuse to move; he may be tapped on his side either with a crop or with the end of the lead rope and told once more firmly to 'walk on.'

- The whip should be used *immediately* the horse shows any resistance. He should not be allowed to have a 'tug of war' as this teaches him bad habits. A firm response to his misbehaviour is essential for future discipline.

- The horse must walk forward actively. If he plods or ambles along, immediately encourage him to walk forward energetically by telling him again in a firm voice to 'Walk On' and by taking quicker, more determined steps beside him.

Trotting in Hand

To trot in hand the horse must first be *walking actively*. Then, taking quicker steps beside him, give the firm instruction to 'Trot on'. Again the whip must be used if the horse does not go forward willingly.

Turning in Hand

This must be performed at the walk. The turn must be made with the handler on the *outside* of the horse

Figure 34: On the nearside turn to the right.

Figure 35: On the offside turn to the left.

This helps the horse to balance himself correctly and prevents him from swinging his hindquarters out, possibly slipping. It also minimizes the risk of him treading on the handler's feet.

Exam Tip

At some point in the practical section, one candidate in the group will be requested to put a headcollar on a horse in the stable and to comment on the fit. Another candidate will tie the horse up with a quick release knot. If there is no string attached to the ring the candidate may point this out to the examiner.

After this the examiner will usually ask one person within the group to lead the horse out of the stable and stand him up correctly for inspection. You may be requested to lead the horse in hand at walk, possibly trot and to execute a turn.

In preparation for the exam practise leading a horse, turning correctly and making him walk and trot *actively*.

C H A P T E R   8
Grooming

Grooming is part of the daily routine of a stabled horse. In a field-kept horse this is slightly different to suit the environment, weather, time of year and workload.

Reasons for Grooming

Good health Grooming is a necessary part of the horse's welfare. Removing waste products, such as sweat, grease, dust, dead skin and hair, it helps to keep the pores open and clean whilst encouraging good blood circulation.

Prevent disease It helps to prevent many skin diseases and infections caused by dust and dirt. It also discourages parasites as they feed on dead hair and skin

Condition It is a form of massage which improves muscle and skin tone.

Appearance Grooming helps to keep the horse clean, healthy and well toned.

Cleanliness It also helps to keep the tack and clothing clean, preventing sores and infections.

Contact The daily grooming session develops a rapport between handler and horse.

Soundness The handler has time and opportunity to inspect the horse closely and thoroughly.

Grooming Equipment

All who work with or own horses should have their own grooming kit. This is much more efficient than constantly asking to borrow someone else's. It is also more hygienic as other people's grooming equipment may be dirty or spread infection and disease.

A grooming box or container

This needs to be fairly sturdy, spacious, easily cleaned and portable. Grooming boxes can be expensive but there are a variety on the market. Some are strong enough to stand on; handy when plaiting the mane. Alternatives, such as a nappy container or baby utility box, are just as suitable. It must be kept clean, well maintained, organised and out of harm's way, especially when grooming the horse.

Hoof pick

These include the folding type, the pick and brush or ordinary pick. The point of the pick should be blunt to prevent damaging the foot. Hoof picks are made of metal or plastic. Some have brightly coloured handles that are easily seen if dropped in the bedding. For a dark coloured pick a good tip is to tie some colourful string to the handle or paint it a bright colour.

Figure 36: Ordinary Pick and Pick & Brush.

Dandy brush

This is used on the coat of an unclipped or coarse-coated horse to remove mud and sweat. The dandy brush is too harsh for a thin-coated or sensitive horse. The dandy should not be used on non-muscular, bony parts of the horse, or on the tail.

Figure 37: Dandy Brush.

Body brush

This is the brush used most often when grooming the horse. Due to its close, fine fibres it cleans deep down to the skin. Types vary from brushes with stiffer bristles for horses with thick, coarse coats to softer brushes for horses with fine hair and sensitive skins.

Figure 38: Body Brush.

Water brush

Similar to a dandy but with softer bristles, the water brush is used either for damping down and laying the mane and tail or for scrubbing off the horse's hooves. This brush can also be useful for removing mud from the sensitive parts of the body such as the hocks.

Figure 39: Water Brush.

Rubber curry comb

This can be used in two ways; in conjunction with the body brush, (although less effective than the metal curry comb), or directly on the horse's body.

The body brush is used on the horse and afterwards swept over the curry comb to remove dirt and grease from the bristles. The dirt on the curry comb should then be removed by banging the comb on the floor of the stable.

Figure 40: Rubber Curry Comb.

On the horse's body the curry comb is used in a circular movement removing mud or sweat and bringing scurf to the surface. Excellent for removing loose hair when the coat is changing. It also encourages circulation by its massaging action.

Curry combs can also be made of plastic, in which case the comb has many small spikes. This type should only be used on heavy coated or thick skinned horses and ponies.

The metal curry comb

In conjunction with the body brush this is used in the same way as the rubber curry comb; the brush being wiped across it between strokes. To use this curry comb efficiently; hold the handle in the palm of the hand with the body of the comb laid back along the wrist. The brush can then be rhythmically stroked across the comb with no possibility of skinning the knuckles. *The metal curry comb should never be used on the horse.*

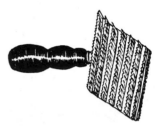

Figure 41: Metal Curry Comb.

Mane and tail comb

There are two sizes of comb; a large one for combing, and a smaller, thinner type used for pulling the mane and tail or as an aid in plaiting. Combs can either be made from metal or plastic.

When cleaning out the tail it is preferable to use a body brush as the comb will split or break the hair.

Sponges

These are essential for cleaning the eyes, nostrils, dock area, sheaths or udders. Sponges can also be used to wash off mud or for wiping the saddle and girth area if sweaty. For hygiene, different sponges should be kept, one for the eyes and nostrils and another for the dock area. To avoid getting these mixed up, use different coloured sponges.

Hoof oil or ointment

The thick, black hoof oil is not so popular now as it may prevent the natural osmotic action of the horn - the free exchange of moisture to and from the hoof. There are many ointments on the market or a simple vegetable oil, such as Soya, Linseed or Olive is just as effective. An old, clean paint brush is ideal for use with hoof ointment.

Scissors

Blunt, curved scissors are used for trimming the bottom of the tail and the whiskers. The mane should never be cut or trimmed with scissors as the growth will become too thick and the mane stand on end. The method of pulling the mane to shorten it also thins it, encouraging it to lie on one side.

Hay wisp or leather massage pad

Traditionally a wisp was made out of hay or straw but now massage pads or gloves are available. These tone up the horse's muscles and improve the circulation. They are used by banging down on the muscular parts of the neck, shoulder and hindquarters. Learning to wisp correctly is important; misuse can cause irritation or actual physical injury to the horse.

Stable rubber

A soft cloth or old clean tea towel wiped over the horse after grooming gives a final polish to the coat and removes any remaining dust.

Sweat scraper

Normally used to remove surplus water from the horse after washing off or bathing, the sweat scraper can also be used for a horse that is sweaty.

Towels

Clean towels are useful for drying off the horse either after bathing or if the legs are wet.

Grooming Machines

Some Yards have grooming machines, of which there are various types on the market. Though these save time and labour, they can be expensive to purchase. A grooming machine should not be used daily but every four to seven days.

Tail bandage

This bandage is applied after grooming to help shape and tidy the horse's tail. Tail bandages are usually made of an elasticated material and can be bought in almost any colour.

Tail bandages, as well as being used during grooming are also useful on other occasions:

- Protection when travelling.

- Shaping the tail after being dampened or washed.

- Keeping the tail out of wet, muddy conditions during activities such as polo or eventing.

- In the case of a reflective tail bandage, as a warning to motorists when riding in dark conditions.

Other Items

Other items useful in a grooming kit are Vaseline and fly repellent. Good quality fly repellent is preferable as cheap ones do not work as well.

Care of Kit

The grooming kit should always be kept clean and in good repair. A dirty kit will not clean the horse efficiently, will deteriorate quickly and may spread disease, infections or cause skin problems. The brushes should be washed regularly in warm water and a mild unscented soap. All metal parts must be kept clean and dry. Bandages must be washed, dried and rolled ready for use. All sponges need cleaning thoroughly in a mild antiseptic solution.

Tail Bandages

Putting On

Check first that the bandage is rolled up correctly with the tapes on the inside. Tie the horse up with a head collar and lead rope. If dealing with a strange or awkward horse, ask an assistant to help.

Pat the horse on the shoulder and continue to stroke and talk to him whilst approaching his hindquarters. If the horse's tail is suddenly grabbed from behind, he could kick.

Damp down the top of the tail with a moistened water brush to make the bandaging easier.

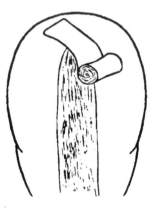

Standing square at the back of the horse, place about four to six inches of the bandage above the tail on horse's hindquarters. The roll of the bandage should be on top. If the roll is underneath it is much more difficult to wind around the tail.

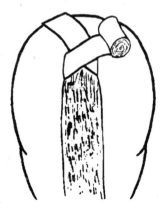

Lift up the tail with the left hand if starting to the right, vice versa if rolling to the left is easier, and roll the bandage under the dock as far up as possible. This is the difficult part, keeping the bandage high enough without it slipping. Practice does help.

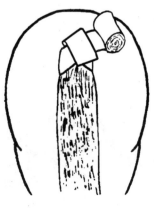

Roll the bandage around the dock twice, firmly. Turn the flap down and roll the bandage over the flap.

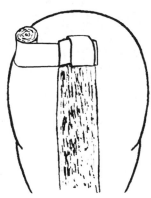

Gradually roll the bandage downwards around the tail, overlapping to approximately half a width, until just above the end of the dock bones. These can easily be felt.

The bandage now travels up the tail until the tapes are reached. Wrap the tapes around the tail and tie them on the outside. Twist the end of the tapes into the bandage to keep them safe, out of the way and tidy. Get hold of the tail and slightly bend it into the shape of horse's rump.

When travelling the tapes can be tied to one side of the tail in case the horse rubs on the back of the trailer and manages to unfasten the tapes.

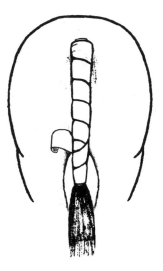

Ideally a well-bandaged tail should have *no hair sticking out of the top*, *look tidy* and have an *even tension*. The tension of the bandage should be tight enough to prevent slipping.

The tapes should never be tighter than the tail bandage. As this will damage one particular area causing a pressure point.

The tail bandage should not be left on for too long a period and should certainly **not** remain on all night. It should never be applied when wet, because when it dries it will contract and tighten.

In the above two cases the blood supply to the dock bones will be impaired; the horse will either end up with white hairs in his tail or he could lose his tail altogether.

The tail bandage can be left on for up to four hours. After this it should be removed and the tail massaged to restore the circulation. When travelling long distances a tail guard is a good substitute for the bandage.

Removing the bandage.

To remove; simply undo the tapes, hold the top of the tail bandage and slide it down the tail until it comes away. The bandage should be washed, thoroughly dried and rolled up ready to be used again.

Exam Tip

Each candidate should be familiar with the grooming kit. During the Stage I you will be given one piece from the kit; asked to name it and describe its use.

At some point during the session on grooming you will have to put on a tail bandage. Tail bandaging does need practice. In an exam situation fingers seem to turn into thumbs and the bandage takes on a life of its own, springing away at the slightest chance and rolling around in the bedding! Try practising with curtains at home, if there is no handy horse tail available.

CHAPTER 9
Grooming Techniques

There are three types of grooming; **'Strapping'**, **'Quartering'**, and **'Brushing Off'**. 'Strapping' is the thorough grooming given daily, usually after the horse has worked. The skin is warm and, because the pores are still open, dirt and grease are easier to remove. 'Quartering' is the quick clean given first thing in the morning before exercise and 'brushing off' is the final grooming of the day. This chapter also covers bathing the horse, washing the mane and tail and cleaning the sheath.

Strapping

Strapping can take from twenty minutes up to one hour depending on the speed, efficiency and thoroughness of the groom. Fitter horses are easier to keep clean because they sweat less.

Method

Prepare the grooming kit and tie up the horse. If the horse is wearing a rug, this can be removed unless the weather is very cold.

The sequence for strapping is:

- Picking out and cleaning the feet.

- Brushing the body.

- Brushing the mane and tail.

- Cleaning the head.

- Sponging the eyes, nostrils, dock, sheath or udders.

- Wisping.

- Oiling the hooves.

- Finishing off.

Picking out the feet

The feet should be cleaned in the same rotation each time to teach the horse a routine. The sequence usually starts with the near fore and the near hind, then the off fore and off hind. Most horses do learn to pick up each foot in readiness. When changing sides, walk around the front of the horse

Method

Tie the horse up safely.

A small skip or bucket is placed behind each foot in turn so that the dirt falls into it and is easily cleared away. This keeps the bedding clean or, if picking out the feet in the yard, saves having to sweep the dirt up afterwards.

Starting with the near fore leg; hold the hoofpick in the right hand, stroke the horse's shoulder with the left and continue down the back of the leg to the fetlock. The horse should pick up his foot automatically. If he does not, squeeze the fetlock gently and tell him to pick up his foot. If he still refuses, lean against his shoulder until he complies. Hold the underneath of the hoof in the left hand and use the pick in the right.

The action of the hoof pick should be in the direction of heel to toe. Bringing the pick upwards towards the heel can prick and damage the frog.

Use the pick down each side of the frog and round the inside of the hoof wall. Clean the central and lateral clefts of the frog carefully. The lateral clefts are the two grooves each side of the frog.

As much dirt as possible should be removed from under the shoe. If the hoof pick has a brush this can be used to clear away remaining dirt.

If necessary, the foot can now be scrubbed with a wet water brush. Keeping the hollow between the heels dry by protecting it with the thumb; scrub the sole and frog gently.

To clean the hind leg, begin by patting the horse on the shoulder and continue to run a hand down the horse's body to the hindquarters. This will give the horse ample warning and prevent him from being startled and perhaps kicking. Continue stroking down the hind leg to the fetlock. Now *pass the hand in front of the leg and hold the hoof from the inside*. This will prevent an injured or broken arm if the horse kicks.

Whilst picking out, carefully inspect each foot for injuries and diseases such as thrush. Thrush is an infection in the foot that can detected by a foul smell and a moist, black discharge around the frog.

Check also that the shoes are secure.

When placing the horse's foot down, control it so that the horse does not drop it with a bang or hit his other leg.

Allow time for the feet to dry before applying any hoof ointment.

When picking out the horse's feet, the handler's back should be kept as straight as possible. This prevents strain or injury should the horse snatch his foot away quickly.

Brushing

The horse is now prepared for brushing.

Caked mud or dried sweat marks can be removed with the dandy brush unless the horse is thin skinned or clipped. Wet mud or sweat must never be brushed as this causes skin problems such as mud fever. Wash the mud off or wait until it dries and brush clean. The rubber curry comb used in a circular motion removes dried mud efficiently and is a good alternative to the Dandy.

The dandy brush is stroked very carefully over the sensitive parts; the belly, loins and lower legs. It is never used on the horse's head.

Body brushing always starts on the nearside of the horse. If the horse's mane falls to the left, lay it over to the other side. Begin at the poll and with the brush in the *left hand* (in order to put body weight into the strokes) and the curry comb in the *right*, clean down the neck. The body brush is used with short strokes in the same direction as the lay of the coat.

Keeping the arm fairly stiff but with the elbow slightly bent, *thoroughly* brush the neck, crest and shoulder area. Use the brush gently when reaching bony or ticklish spots such as knees, hocks and the girth area.

The horse can be brushed in the following sequence:

1. Poll to withers to include shoulders and chest.

2. Barrel, back and loins.

3. Hindquarters.

4. Girth area and belly.

5. Foreleg.

6. Hind leg.

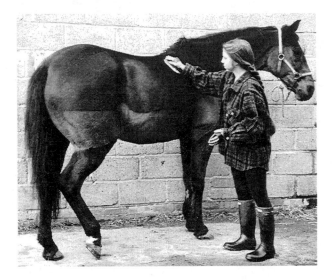

The body brush should be frequently cleaned by sweeping it across the rubber or metal curry comb. This is done after every four or five strokes. If the brush is cleaned after every stroke, not only is it strenuous and time-consuming, but the brush deteriorates and wears out more quickly. Tap the comb on the floor to remove the dirt.

On the offside repeat the procedure with the brush in the *right hand* and the curry comb in the *left*.

Mane

Starting at the withers and working up towards the poll, brush the mane a few locks at a time. If possible encourage the lay of the mane to the *right hand* side of the neck by using a dampened water brush. There is often confusion as to which is the correct side to lay the mane. Traditionally the mane should lie to the right but with some horses the mane falls naturally to the left.

Tail

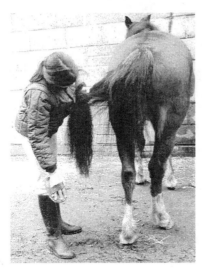

Holding the tail in one hand and working a few strands at a time, very gently brush out bedding and tangles with a soft body brush.

Thin or fine tails can be cleaned by finger combing when the bedding is removed by running the fingers through the hair rather than the brush.

To tease out really stubborn knots use a mane and tail comb gently. Never pull the comb through as this will break the hair and the horse will end up with a thin tail. A body brush is used on the bony part of the tail to remove scurf.

Tail Bandage

With a wet water brush dampen the tail slightly and put on the tail bandage.

Cleaning the head

This should be done very gently. Undo the headcollar and fasten it around the horse's neck, leaving the head free. *Unfasten the quick release knot and leave the leadrope hanging through the string. This prevents the headcollar from damaging the horse's neck should he pull back suddenly.* Using a hand to steady the head, very gently brush around the face, avoiding the eyes or nostrils.

With a head shy or nervous horse it may be safer to leave the headcollar on with the leadrope untied and left through the string as described.

Sponging

Using a damp sponge, gently wipe the eyes and nose. With a different sponge clean the dock, sheath or udder. Dry off these areas in winter with a towel to prevent chapping.

Gently clean the eyes, nostrils, dock, sheath or udders with a sponge and tepid water. An application of Vaseline to the dock or udders helps to keep these areas soft and pliable.

Wisping

This part of strapping is rarely done in busy yards as it is time consuming. There are also those who believe that wisping may damage the muscle fibres. Others consider it is beneficial to the horse to be given a weekly wisping, as a form of massage, developing and hardening the muscles. It produces a beautiful shine on the coat by drawing oil from the glands and stimulates the skin by increasing the blood circulation. Traditionally wisps are made from hay, but leather massage pads or gloves are now available and can be used instead.

Wisping is performed quite vigorously so it is wise to find out first whether or not the horse will accept this action.

If made of hay, damp down the wisp slightly, and use it by slapping it on the muscular part of the horse's body. Bang it strongly in the direction of the coat about a dozen times. Do not wisp the horse's head, any bony parts or the tender loin region.

Oiling the Hooves

The dry hooves can now be oiled. There are hoof oils and ointment on the market that can be used for weak or split hooves. The sole and frog can be oiled as well.

Finishing off

Finally, wipe over the horse with a stable rubber. This gives a final polish removing any remaining dust. The stable rubber can be damped down if required.

Quartering

This term traditionally refers to the method of grooming given to horses when wearing a rug. The front buckles are unfastened and the rug pulled back from the withers onto the hindquarters. The two front 'quarters', left and right, are groomed. The rug is then replaced onto the forehand and the back part of the rug folded over onto the front; the two hind 'quarters' are cleaned. This type of grooming can therefore be achieved without removing the roller or surcingles.

Quartering now refers to the grooming performed in the morning usually before work. This is a condensed form of strapping and usually takes about ten to twenty minutes.

The procedure for quartering is as follows:

- Pick out the feet.
- Brush the body.
- Clean the Mane and Tail.
- Sponge eyes, nostrils and dock.

The purpose of quartering is to remove the dirt accumulated overnight and to clean the horse ready for exercise. Bedding, straw or shavings are brushed off the body and out of the mane and tail. Stable stains need to be cleaned, particularly on grey horses and ponies. Unless the weather is freezing a damp brush can be used or, for really stubborn stains, a damp sponge,

Brushing Off

The horse is given a quick clean and brush down before he retires for the night.

The feet are picked out; the horse given a quick brushing over and the eyes, nostrils and dock sponged. In winter the rugs should not be removed completely except if changing to a night rug.

Grooming the Grass Kept Horse or Pony

For the horse or pony permanently at grass, the amount and frequency of grooming is different. Whilst daily attention is necessary, particularly with regard to the feet, full grooming depends on the time of year, the weather conditions and the need for insulation.

Daily Care

The feet need picking out every day. Hoof oil or ointment can also be applied.

Grooming can be done daily during spring, summer and early autumn. This grooming resembles Quartering or Brushing Off more than Strapping because the horse needs to keep a certain amount of oil, grease and even dust in the coat to endure wet, windy or cold weather. After brushing, a coating with a fly repellent is an excellent idea. The eyes, nose, dock, sheath or udder should be cleaned regularly.

Winter Care

In the winter months insulation is vital. Though the feet need picking out daily; during this time a quick brush down before exercise is all that is needed. The mane and tail can be brushed. Sponging is not advisable during very cold or freezing weather. Horses and ponies at grass still need to be kept relatively clean and examined every day for injuries, cuts, bruises, swellings, sores or thorns.

After exercise care

After exercise any dirty areas on the horse or pony should be cleaned. If the horse or pony is very sweaty this can either be cleaned by hosing in summer or with a sponge in winter. *All wet areas should be dried scrupulously with a towel before the horse or pony is put back into the field*

With grass kept horses and ponies, it is essential to keep a balance between cleanliness and the need for insulation. It is important to keep the feet in good condition, to examine for any problems and to allow time for contact with humans, so vital for the horse and pony permanently out at pasture.

Safety Points Whilst Grooming

1. Never stand directly behind the horse.

2. Never sit or kneel beside the horse when grooming the lower parts. Always bend or squat.

3. Never place hands on the floor, the horse may tread on them.

4. Never crawl under the horse's belly to reach the other side, no matter how well you know the horse!

5. Never lean in front of the hind leg when brushing the sheath or udder area. Horses can be very ticklish here and may kick.

When not to groom

As mentioned above horses and ponies out at grass, particularly during the winter, should not be given a thorough daily groom.

In addition ill or invalid horses are not usually given a strapping, particularly if very ill, as they need peace and quiet. A very light brushing or even just wiping the eyes, nose and dock area with a warm, damp sponge will suffice.

Bathing the horse

Horses are occasionally given a bath; in spring to remove any remaining winter coat or in the summer to improve the appearance before a Show. They may also be bathed for medical reasons; to help skin problems heal properly.

Horses however should not be bathed too frequently as this will remove vital oils and grease, making the coat and skin dry and scaly. A horse should not be given a bath on a cold day, even on a warm or hot day bathing should be completed as early as possible to prevent the horse getting a chill.

Bathe with warm water if possible or, if the horse will accept it, cold water from a hose pipe. A horse shampoo or baby shampoo is suitable as long as it is unscented.

When using warm water, begin at the poll and wet the neck. With a hose pipe start at the feet and gradually move up the legs and body, allowing the horse to become accustomed to the cold water. If the horse hollows his back when the cold water is applied, stop and use a sponge.

Continue down the length of the body and apply the shampoo. (The horse can be washed in sections rather than all the body at once.) Build up a good lather by rubbing with the hands or a rubber mitt. The mane can also be washed at this time.

Rinse off thoroughly. It is important that all the shampoo is washed out completely or it may cause irritation to the skin. Start at the top of the horse's body and rinse down towards the legs. Repeat the process on the opposite side.

Using the sweat scraper in long sweeps, remove excess water from the horse's body. Dry the lower legs with towels and, if possible, put a sweat rug on the horse and walk him until dry.

The head is washed using clear water only, *no soap*. Remove the headcollar and fasten it around the horse's neck. Wet the head gently with a sponge taking care that no water gets inside the ears.

Washing the Mane

As well as being washed with the rest of the body the mane is often washed on its own.

Tie up the horse correctly with headcollar and lead rope. Prepare warm water, horse shampoo, a large sponge, towels and a sweat scraper.

Starting at the forelock, avoiding the eyes and ears, wet the mane with the sponge and thoroughly rub in the shampoo. Rinse with warm water making sure that all the soap is removed. Sweep away any surplus water with the sweat scraper. Dry with a towel and brush out the mane with a clean brush.

Washing the Tail

Soak the tail by immersing as much of it as possible into a bucket of water. Take care when the water reaches the dock area, particularly if the water is cold!

Wet the top part of the tail with a sponge. Apply the shampoo and rub in thoroughly. Wash around the dock area to remove scurf. Rinse the soap out completely.

Dry the tail by holding it half way up and, standing to one side, swish the lower part of the tail around in a circle. Some horses do object to this action so be prepared to stop immediately should the horse become upset.

Dry the dock area with a towel.

Brush out the tail gently with a clean brush and apply a tail bandage.

Washing the Sheath

The sheath should be washed regularly; if neglected it becomes infected, sore and the horse may experience difficulty in passing water. Dirt in the sheath can also cause a noise when the horse is moving, (though this is also due to trapped air in the sheath, an indication that the horse is tense).

An assistant may be necessary to hold the horse.

Prepare a bucket of warm water, a mild, non-scented soap or sheath wash and a rubber glove. Instead of soap, some water with a small amount of antiseptic can be used.

Approach the horse correctly from the neck and shoulder and stroke him along the back to his hindquarters. Place the glove on one hand and immerse this hand into the bucket of water. Apply the soap to the glove. Gently insert the gloved hand into the sheath and wash, carefully picking off bits of dirt and grit. If preferred, a sponge can be used in the same way. Thoroughly clean the glove or sponge afterwards.

Exam Tip

During the grooming session the group will be divided, into individuals or pairs. Each will be given one grooming kit and instructed to groom a stabled horse, put on a tail bandage, pick out and inspect the horse's feet. Before starting to groom, restrain the horse correctly first. Do not groom with gloves on as you need to feel and inspect the horse's body for injuries, wounds or swellings.

The examiner may ask questions about grooming procedures, the different types of grooming methods, the time each takes and when each is performed. The Examiner may also ask about grooming grass-kept horses and ponies and when not to groom.

C H A P T E R 10
Bedding

For stabled horses or for those spending short periods in a box or stall, bedding is put down on the floor and used for several reasons;

1. To prevent the **jarring** effect on the feet and legs of a horse standing for hours on a hard surface.

2. To provide **insulation, warmth** and **protection** from draughts.

3. To encourage the horse to **stale.**

4. To allow the horse to **roll and rest** in comfort.

5. To prevent the horse from **slipping and falling**.

Types of Bedding

Straw

This is the traditional type of bedding. It has a number of advantages and disadvantages:

✓ Easy to obtain.	✗ Labour intensive. There are no short cuts with a straw bed, it must be mucked out thoroughly each day.
✓ Economical to buy.	
✓ The bales are convenient to store	✗ Straw may be eaten by the horse.
✓ Permits free drainage, as long as the stable floor has drainage outlets.	✗ Can be dusty or contain fungal spores causing respiratory problems.
✓ Makes a bright, comfortable, warm bed.	✗ May be difficult to obtain good straw constantly. There is no guarantee of good quality so the buyer must always be more observant to avoid bad straw.

Figure 42: Straw Bed.

There are three types of straw.

1. **Wheat** is the best type and the one most commonly in use.

2. **Oat** is very palatable and likely to be eaten by the horse. It is also quite porous and tends to become saturated and heavy.

3. **Barley** straw is palatable and, though modern farming methods are making this less likely, it may contain sharp ears or awns irritating to the horse's skin.

Figure 43: Woodchip & Straw Bales.

Woodshavings or Wood chip

As the name implies this is chippings or shavings of wood packed into plastic bags, sometimes called bales. There are several varieties to choose from including large wood chip or softer, finer shavings. The bales are also available in different sizes, from the smaller bale of 20 to 25 kgs, extending to the larger bales of 30 to 35 kgs.

✓ Economical.	✗ A bed of shavings needs to be kept very clean as it is quite porous. It quickly becomes soggy and dark in colour. Droppings and soiled patches need to be removed frequently.
✓ Easy to obtain	
✓ Makes a bright, comfortable bed.	
✓ Labour and time saving if kept clean and droppings removed frequently.	✗ Cannot be disposed of easily.
✓ Will not be eaten by the horse.	✗ Not quite as comfortable as straw unless a very thick bed is laid.
✓ Good for horses with respiratory problems.	✗ Not as warm as straw because there is no trapped air.

Peat moss

This can provide a comfortable bed but needs cleaning frequently.

✓ This bedding is not palatable.	✗ Expensive to buy.
✓ There are no dust or spores.	✗ Becomes very soggy and heavy.
✓ It does not burst into flame so is particularly useful where there is a risk of fire.	✗ Tends to be very dark in appearance.
	✗ Can be difficult to dispose of even though it is an excellent garden manure when rotted.

Shredded Paper

This bedding consists of paper pieces.

✓ It is dust free, beneficial for horses affected by stable dust. ✓ Inexpensive to buy.	✗ Being absorbent, paper becomes very heavy when saturated which makes it difficult to muck out. ✗ When dry the paper can blow about the yard in windy conditions. ✗ Shredded paper is often made from old printed newspaper which may leave stains on the horse, particularly a grey.

Rubber matting

Common in trailers and horse boxes, rubber matting is being used more often as a stable bedding. It can either be used on its own or with other bedding material on top.

✓ When used on its own it is obviously dust free. ✓ Is very easy to muck out as the dung is removed and urine cleaned by hose pipe. ✓ After the initial outlay there is no other bedding to buy, so upkeep can be cheap.	✗ It does not allow the horse to lie or roll in comfort, if at all. ✗ It can appear revolting when not cleaned properly and the dung is trampled around by the horse. ✗ There is often a smell from the ammonia fumes. ✗ Urine often streams out into the yard. ✗ The stable needs good drainage to allow the urine to drain away. ✗ It can offer little warmth. ✗ There are no banks for insulation, to protect from draughts or to prevent the horse from becoming cast.

Deep Litter

This is not a type of bedding but a method of keeping a bed, usually with straw or shavings. Initially the bed is made very deep and only mucked out completely every three to six months. Soiled or damp patches and dung are taken out regularly and clean bedding placed on top.

This method is labour saving initially and provides a deep, warm bed. When the full mucking out has to be done though, it takes a long time and is very heavy work. The box then needs to be dried out thoroughly.

The deep litter method is rapidly declining in popularity. It is now thought that problems are caused by the fungal spores which thrive in the constantly warm, damp conditions.

New ideas for bedding occasionally appear on the market but the above are the most usual types. The decision about the type of bedding to use depends on several factors. The first consideration is the horse, whether he is likely to eat the bedding or if he suffers from respiratory problems. Other factors include cost, convenience of storage, disposal, management of the yard and personal preference. Straw is the most popular but is unsuitable for some horses, in which case shavings or shredded paper are better.

Keeping the Bed Clean

A stabled horse may be standing for long periods on the bedding, sometimes as long as twenty-three hours a day. In this time he will pass droppings, urinate, lie down, roll and sometimes eat the bedding. For hygiene and his physical well-being, the bed must be regularly cleared of wet, soiled patches and dung.

A dirty neglected bed can cause serious problems. The horse may eat the soiled bedding and suffer from colic. There is a greater likelihood of worm infestation from the dung. Vermin and insects will thrive in warm damp conditions. The box will certainly smell offensive and if the walls of the box are wooden they will rot. The horse may suffer skin irritations; any scratches, grazes or wounds on his body will become dirty and infected. It will definitely be more difficult to keep the horse clean.

Bedding is cleaned by 'Skipping Out', 'Mucking Out' and 'Bedding Down'.

Skipping Out

At frequent intervals during the day, dung is removed from the bed using a fork and skip. Ideally it should be done every time a horse passes droppings, but at least three times a day. This not only keeps the bed clean but also makes mucking out easier.

A quicker method of skipping out, particularly with shavings, is to remove the droppings by hand. Rubber gloves should be worn.

Mucking Out

Performed once a day, usually in the morning, this involves the complete removal of dung and soiled bedding.

All the necessary tools are prepared; a fork (pitchfork, four or five-pronged fork or shavings fork depending on the bedding) skip, mucking out sheet, bucket or wheel barrow, brush and shovel. The horse should be restrained with a head collar and lead rope either in the box or ideally outside.

All dung is removed together with the heavily soiled patches. Dried bedding is separated from the remaining wet areas and tossed to the side of the box. Straw needs to be shaken with the fork to reveal the dirty bedding. With shavings, wet patches can be distinguished by colour and weight - these are either a deep golden or a dark brown colour, very heavy and may be stuck together.

The clean bedding and banks at the sides of the box are sifted through with the fork to remove any remaining droppings. The floor is brushed clean. On warm days bedding can be piled against the walls of the box to allow the stable floor to dry.

To lay the bed, the old bedding is put down and new bedding, thoroughly shaken out, placed on top. The banks around the sides of the box are built up high and wide, then levelled by skimming the fork across the top. The bed is also flattened down by skimming the fork across it. This is particularly necessary for shavings in order to create a level bed. The edges of the bed by the door and any other clear areas are tidied with the brush. All muck is removed by wheel barrow or muck sheet to the muck heap and the tools put away properly.

At regular intervals, every four to six weeks, the floor can be treated with a disinfectant. Both floor and walls need regular treatment to kill off any disease or infection and to remove offensive odours. Some products are available which, when sprinkled on the floor, get rid of all offensive smells. These are effective but can be expensive.

Bedding Down

In the evening the bed needs to be cleaned and tidied once more.

Dung and soiled patches are removed. More bedding is laid down as a night bed. There are two types of bed, the day and the night bed. The day bed should be deep enough to be comfortable. The night bed is deeper as the horse will be standing on this for some 8 - 12 hours.

To test the depth of the night bed gently let the fork drop, points first, into the bed. These should not hit the floor. If the fork can be heard hitting the ground then the bed is not deep enough.

Setting Fair.

Another term used with regard to the stable area is 'setting fair'. This means cleaning the area within and around the box. Brushing and clearing away all dust and bedding in the yard area, and generally tidying away tools and equipment.

Banks.

Wide, high banks are laid against the walls, usually the two side walls and the back wall. The banks should be one to two feet in height above the bed, of an even thickness and level along the top. Droppings and soiled bedding should always be cleaned out and never left in the banks.

Figure 44: Banks in a Woodchip Bed.

Banks are important with all types of bedding:

1. To prevent the horse becoming cast.

    Sometimes when a horse rolls or lies down, his legs become trapped against the wall. In this situation he cannot either roll over or push himself up, he is 'cast'. The horse may then panic, go into shock or injure himself. Banks help to prevent this predicament; they stop the horse from getting too close to the walls and give his legs some leverage should he lie down or roll.

2. To provide insulation against cold and draughts.

A correctly laid bed will be clean, warm, soft and free from sharp objects, with the banks tidy and level. The whole box will provide the horse with a comfortable, safe and warm environment in which to live.

Muck Heaps

Another important part of yard management is the keeping of the muck heaps. A yard can be judged by its muck heaps. If this area is well managed, kept clean, tidy and hygienically controlled; then the rest of the establishment should be efficiently run.

Ideally there should be three muck heaps;

1. One that is well rotted and ready to take away.
2. One in the process of rotting.
3. One in use.

Daily care is needed to keep the muck heap correctly. The new muck should be put on the appropriate heap and forked into shape. Various yards have different methods of building the heap. Some prefer heaps built in steps; others prefer squares with vertical sides. Whichever method is used the correct stacking of muck is essential for tidiness, hygiene and to allow the manure to rot properly. There should be no muck left lying around or blowing about the yard; the whole area should be frequently cleaned, brushed and set fair.

It is ideal to have the heap in an enclosed area such as a square, walled on three sides, perhaps with a ramp for wheelbarrows and the open side a convenient access for lorries.

Site of the Heap

The position of the muck heap in relation to the yard is vital. This should be at a convenient distance for the stable hands carrying or wheeling muck; yet not too close constituting a health threat or a possible fire hazard should the heap overheat or be burnt deliberately. If laid against wooden buildings or boxes, the damp muck will rot the walls.

Heaps should be situated down wind from the yard to minimize any unpleasant smells and, if possible, kept out of sight. A muck heap by the side of the driveway into the stables is not a pretty sight, particularly if it is not kept well!

If the yard is situated in hilly country, ideally the muck heap should be positioned down hill. The workers will not then have to haul the muck uphill. All heaps should have an access that is easy and dry, even better if the access is made of concrete. There is nothing worse than trying to push a loaded wheelbarrow up a steep, muddy track to the heap in cold, wet weather!

Disposing of muck these days is not easy. Many farmers do not require shavings and even disposing of straw may be difficult, though gardeners still like to use horse manure (especially for roses)!

It is definitely not a good idea to spread muck over fields to be grazed by horses. This does not encourage the growth of the right type of grasses and there is also the danger of spreading worms and their larvae.

A well-managed yard will have efficiently run Muck Heaps.

Stable Construction

This subject is not included in the syllabus for Stage I, but occasionally Examiners will ask basic questions about stables or boxes; size, construction, materials, fixtures and fittings.

Size

'I still say she needs glasses!'

The box must be large enough to accommodate the horse or pony, allowing him to turn around, feed, lie down or roll in comfort. A box size of 12 feet by 14 feet will accommodate the largest horse; 12' by 12' for horses around 16 hands; 10' by 10' for around 15 hands and 8' x 8' for small ponies. Checking the size of a box is done by striding the area. There should be approximately three feet to one stride. A dark box will look smaller.

Height

The box must be of a sufficient height for the horse so that he does not hit his head. The ceiling or roof needs to be from 12 to 15 foot high.

Door

The door should be high and wide enough for the horse to enter and exit without hitting his hips or banging his head. This means a minimum of 4 feet wide and, depending on the size of horse, a height of 10 feet approximately. Doors on pony boxes are often smaller in size. Most stable doors are split to allow the upper portion to be opened for ventilation.

Condition and Ventilation

The box must be waterproof, dry and warm, but without being stuffy. Good ventilation is essential. Horses and ponies do need a good supply of fresh air but there must be no draughts. For this reason the door and window should be on the same side of the box to prevent air streaming through from one side to another. There should be kicking boards all round.

Floor

The floor should allow drainage towards the back of the box. A horse should never have to stand in a pool of water and urine stagnating at the doorway. The floor needs to be strong enough to withstand wear and tear from four shod hooves. It should not be slippery.

Fixtures and Fittings

These should be kept to an *absolute minimum*. If there is anything on which the horse can catch himself, hurt, injure or wound himself then that is precisely what he will do (usually the night before a major competition or outing)!

Essential fittings are; two securing rings on which to tie the horse and haynet; a device for water, either an automatic water bowl or water bucket and some extremely safe lighting.

The securing rings should have string attached to which the horse can be tied. If water is given in a bucket it must be set in a safe, static position or placed within a rubber tyre.

If the horse is fed from a feed bucket, this must be removed from the stable immediately after use. If it cannot be removed quickly then it must be made safe by being placed in a rubber tyre. There are alternatives such as the bucket designed to fit over the door or the soft rubber feed skip which will not injure the horse if it is tossed around. A bucket hung from a clip is often used but again it adds another fixture within the stable which may provide a hazard.

Light must be available in the box. It is extremely dangerous not to have light within a stable if the horse is being dealt with after dark. There should be no exposed light bulbs or wiring; these must be adequately protected. All electrical wires must be properly insulated. All electrical components must be completely safe, regularly checked and out of the horse's reach.

Ideally there should be no clips or hooks, projecting nails or screws, no light switches, exposed cables, splintered or rotting wood, glass - anything on which the horse could injure himself.

Fixtures and fittings should be kept to a minimum in the box!

Exam Tip

Before the exam day, take a look at various types of bedding; ask working pupils or owners which type of bedding they prefer and why. Practise describing the various methods of mucking out and laying the bed. Even if this is a daily task it is not always easy to explain in a clear and concise way. The next time you muck out, talk yourself through the various stages; from tying the horse up outside with a haynet, preparing the wheelbarrow and shavings fork to laying the bed down neatly. Often in exams the important point is not how much knowledge you have but how you communicate this to the examiner.

For stable construction practise estimating size, observe the construction and fittings; start assessing boxes critically. Consider possible improvements for safer, more efficient fittings and attachments if any.

C H A P T E R   11
Watering

Horses require both food and water to survive. However, of the two water is more vital. A horse can survive some time without food but will dehydrate and die within days if deprived of water. It is essential for life; all bodily functions need water to work efficiently and chemical reactions within the body take place in a water solution.

A horse's body comprises of approximately 70% water and this is needed for;

- **Digestion** — Lack of water can cause colic particularly if the horse is fed dry foods.

- **Temperature Regulation** — As in sweating where evaporation of moisture from the skin has a cooling effect.

- **Lubrication** — In areas such as joints and eyes.

- **Metabolism** — For the proper working of the chemical reactions in the body.

- **Waste disposal** — As in urine, droppings and sweat.

Water must be available to the horse constantly and it must be clean, free of dirt or pollution. Horses can drink an average of 8 gallons a day, sometimes up to 15 gallons in hot weather. They can be fussy drinkers, refusing tainted water.

The amount of water necessary depends on certain factors;

- **Temperature** — In hot weather the horse will sweat, losing fluids from the body.

- **Work** — Heavy or fast work will also result in sweating and again loss of bodily fluids.

- **Diet** — If the horse is fed dry food and hay he will drink more water.

- **Milk production** — Brood mares need more water to produce the milk for their foals.

- **Faecal and urinary loss** — Diarrhoea results in an abnormal loss of fluids.

Rules of Watering

1. A horse must have a constant supply of clean water.

2. Water utensils and containers must be kept clean.

3. Water before feeding.

4. Do not water when the horse is hot after work.

5. Do not work the horse hard immediately after a deep draught of water.

6. Containers should be large and deep enough to allow a good deep drink.

7. Containers should be safe and sturdy.

When NOT to Water

A horse should NOT be given water:

After a feed

This flushes undigested food out of the stomach. (Though in most cases where the horse has a constant access to water this is not a drastic problem.)

After very hard work when the horse is hot.

Cold water given to a hot horse will cause a shock to the system. Slightly warmer water only should be given until the horse has cooled down sufficiently. The warmer water can be made up by adding some hot water to a bucket of cold water, until the temperature is lukewarm.

Hot or exhausted horses should be given about a quarter of a bucket at a time, approximately every twenty minutes.

Before hard, fast work

The liquid will bloat the stomach and may restrict breathing.

Stagnant, stale, polluted or dirty

Usually horses are fussy and will not drink tainted water. If there is no clean water available though and the horse is thirsty enough, he may drink unsuitable water.

Water in the Stable

There are two main ways in which to water horses in the stable - by bucket or by automatic drinking bowls.

Buckets

The water bucket must be heavy enough so as not to tip over and large enough to allow a deep drink. It should be of strong rubber or plastic; metal is not really suitable. Ideally it should be light enough to be carried even when almost full of water.

A bucket can be secured by a clip on the wall.

A better method is to place the bucket in a rubber tyre on the floor; the horse cannot injure himself or tip the bucket over and decide to play football with it!

✓ Easily cleaned.	✗ Buckets can be extremely heavy and cumbersome to carry around the yard. Not a pleasant job in mid-winter when it is cold and the ground is slippery.
✓ Intake can be monitored.	
✓ Intake can be regulated. The water can be taken away from the horse at times when he should not drink.	✗ Hazardous in the stable if not properly secured.
✓ In winter ice can be removed and the bucket refilled with fresh water.	✗ Labour-intensive and time-consuming; filling, cleaning and refilling.

Automatic Drinking Bowls

This is the most popular method of providing water for the stabled horse. The bowls are usually of metal or fibreglass. They are connected to the water supply and operated by a ball cock method. Horses soon learn to operate them.

Advantages :

✓ Provides a constant supply of clean water.	✗ Can be hard to keep clean unless religiously done every day.
✓ Labour and time saving - can be significant in a large, busy yard.	✗ Metal bowls may rust.
	✗ Some bowls are quite small and do not allow the horse a deep drink.
	✗ Water cannot be regulated.
	✗ Water cannot be monitored.
	✗ Can have a tendency to freeze over in winter, or the pipes may become frozen

Despite the fact that the disadvantages seemingly outweigh the advantages, if properly maintained automatic drinking bowls do work extremely well.

Water In the Field

Water can be provided in three ways within the field; naturally by stream or river, by a trough, or by buckets.

Rivers and Streams

Nowadays it is a sad fact that many rivers and streams are polluted. Even at best there is always a doubt that the water is clean and pure.

The river or stream must have a gravel bed. A sandy bed can cause sand colic as the horse ingests sand in the water. The approach to the drinking area must be kept safe and clean or it can quickly become 'poached', that is churned up by the horses' hooves, muddy, slippery and dangerous.

Any polluted water, dangerous rivers, stagnant pools or ponds, bogs or swamps, poached or dangerous banks must be fenced off and the horse kept away. All these areas are life threatening to the horse.

Troughs

This is a popular method of watering in the field. The most efficient type is the self-filling trough that is connected to the mains water pipe and controlled by a ball cock. The animals can take water whenever they need it. The only problem with this type of trough is that unless the pipes are properly insulated, they can become frozen in winter.

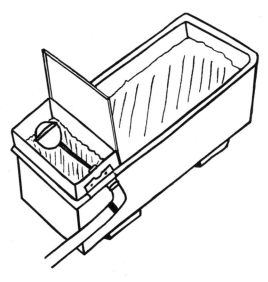

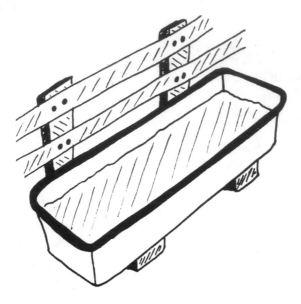

Another container used frequently is the 'bath' trough filled either by buckets or by a hosepipe. Old baths are good water containers if made safe first. All sharp corners must be smoothed and the taps removed altogether. The bath must be kept sufficiently filled with water particularly during hot weather.

The trough should have a good water supply either by a mains pipe, a hosepipe or be at a convenient distance for workers carrying refill buckets.

In winter the water needs to be kept clear of ice. In a trough this can be achieved either by daily breaking the ice or by placing a large rubber ball in the water. The ball floats around preventing the ice forming. (In severe weather daily inspections will be necessary as the water may still freeze over.)

As with all types of water container, the trough must be kept clean. This necessitates regular and frequent emptying, scrubbing and thorough rinsing of the trough.

Site of the trough

The position of a trough is important. It needs to be convenient for the horse without constituting a danger. A trough situated by a fence may either be parallel or at right angles to it. If it is slightly away from a fence, a horse may become stuck behind the  trough leaving him vulnerable to bullying from others.

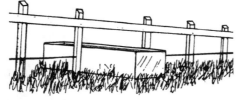

Placed in the middle of the field the trough creates an obstacle that can easily cause injury. A trough should not be placed under deciduous trees; the water will become clogged with leaves, flowers, seeds and twigs.

Approach

The approach to the trough should be kept dry either by laying a concrete or hard-core surround or by covering the ground with straw or shavings. The water trough must be situated well away from gates, muddy areas or hollows, where the ground very quickly becomes poached.

If the trough is regularly and properly maintained it is the most convenient and efficient method of watering in the field.

Buckets

Providing water by buckets in the field can be hard work. It is not a convenient or efficient method, being labour intensive and time consuming. Buckets need to be constantly cleaned and refilled. They can also be kicked over and become a hazard. There are times, however, when buckets must be used in place of other watering systems, which are either inoperative or unavailable.

Exam Tip

In preparation for the exam, inspect various types of watering systems used in stables, farms, yards, fields and boxes. Assess these systems recognizing the positive and negative points.

C H A P T E R 12
Feeding

Correct feeding is essential for the health of the horse. A well-balanced diet should provide all the necessary nutrients to maintain the horse in good condition.

Aims of Feeding

A horse needs food for the following reasons:

1. **To maintain body temperature**

    Maintaining body temperature is important particularly for horses living out in winter.

2. **Growth**

    A variety of nutrients are necessary for growth especially in young stock.

3. **Energy**

    Certain foods are needed to create energy so that the horse can perform his work.

4. **To maintain correct weight**

    Keeping his natural body weight is essential; an underweight or thin horse will find it difficult to keep warm or perform work properly.

5. **Breeding in the case of stallions and brood mares**

    For breeding, stallions need energy and condition; mares need to provide food for the foetus and eventually the foal.

At this point it is as well to mention that overfeeding a horse can be disastrous, resulting in illnesses caused either by obesity or hyperactivity. Here comes another cliché **'the eye of the Master maketh the horse fat.'** In other words doting owners tend to overfeed. Starvation is obviously not beneficial but as a rule it is wiser to underfeed a little rather than overfeed. Of course the ultimate aim is to feed the right amount.

Rules of Feeding

A horse's digestive system is quite finely tuned and, if incorrectly fed, a horse can easily develop digestive disorders which at worse can be fatal. There are certain rules therefore which help to prevent any stress to the system and thus minimize the risk of digestive problems.

The ten rules of feeding are:

1.	**Feed little and often.**	The horse's stomach is small in relation to his size, so food must be given in small amounts at frequent intervals. This will also follow, as closely as possible, the horse's natural lifestyle. Ideally a horse should never go for more than 8 hours without food.
2.	**Plenty of bulk.**	The horse's digestive system needs to be constantly filled to work efficiently. Bulk foods such as hay and grass achieve this.
3.	**Correct amount and type.**	Feeding too much, too little or the wrong type of food can cause physical and mental problems. See Considerations of Feeding.
4.	**Good quality food.**	Inferior foods lack nutritional value and may contain dust.
5.	**Make no sudden change to the diet.**	All alterations to diet must be gradual to avoid digestive problems.
6.	**Do not feed directly before exercise.**	This can cause colic and breathing problems. A horse must be allowed at least one hour after a feed before he is worked.
7.	**Routine.**	Horses are creatures of habit and need to be fed as near as possible at the same time each day.
8.	**Cleanliness.**	All utensils must be kept scrupulously clean.
9.	**A succulent each day.**	Foods such as apples, carrots or swedes add variety to the diet and provide some essential vitamins. Particularly important if the horse is not at grass frequently.
10.	**Water before feeding.**	To prevent undigested food from being washed out of the stomach if the horse drinks after the feed.

Considerations of Feeding

There are three basic elements to feeding; the first is to calculate the **total daily amount** the horse or pony needs. The second is to divide this amount into **concentrates and roughage**. (Concentrates are 'hard' foods, those that provide energy and stamina. Roughage is bulk food, such as hay and chaff). The third element is the **type of food** to give. All three, that is the **amount, percentages** and **type** depend on certain factors.

These will vary according to:

1. The weight of the horse.
2. The breed.
3. Temperament.
4. Amount and type of work.
5. Type of rider.
6. Whether fully stabled or out at grass.
7. Time of year.
8. Type of pasture.
9. Age of the Horse.

Amount

The total daily amount is calculated from the **weight** of the horse. There are four main methods of working out the weight.

i.   A weigh bridge.
The horse is weighed on a special bridge.

ii. A Weigh Tape.
The horse is measured around the barrel, just behind the withers in the girth area.

iii. A Weight Table.
This gives height, build and approximate body weight in kilos and pounds.

iv. Estimation by height.
In practice, the last method is the simplest and easiest to use, unless for specific reasons the horse's diet must be absolutely precise. In the examination, candidates should be able to work out an approximate daily amount from the height.

17 hands = 34 lbs.
16 hands = 30 lbs.
15 hands = 26 lbs.
14 hands = 22 lbs.
13 hands = 18 lbs.
12 hands = 14 lbs.

For those horses and ponies who are half a hand or 2 inches higher, an extra 2 lbs is added. For example a 13.2 hand pony will need 20 lbs.

Estimation of Weight from Height

Here are some simple calculations that may help to remember the above numbers.

Example 1

Multiply height x 2 and deduct 2,4,6,8 or 10.

> **16 hands x 2 - 2 = 30 lbs. (16 x 2 = 32 - 2 = 30)**
> **15 hands x 2 - 4 = 26 lbs. (15 x 2 - 4)**
> **14 hands x 2 - 6 = 22 lbs. (14 x 2 - 6)**
> **13 hands x 2 - 8 = 18 lbs (13 x 2 - 8)**

Example 2

Height - 10 x 4 + 6

For a 15 hand horse:

> **15 - 10 = 5**
> **5 x 4 = 20**
> **20 + 6 = 26**

Example 3

Remember that 12 hands = 14 lbs and add 4 lbs for every additional hand.

Each student and candidate will need to discover which calculation is the easiest to remember. Some will find one way simpler than another, depending on whether they have a good memory or a mathematical brain! Alternatively candidates may choose their own method of working out the amounts.

Variables

Once the total daily amount is worked out there are two points to take into consideration which will affect this amount.

1. The horse's build.

2. If he is kept at grass.

Build

Horses of the same height can vary in build. This often depends on breeding and ancestry. For instance a Thoroughbred will have a tendency to be fine or small boned and will consequently weigh less than a heavy hunter of the same height. The estimate, based on a medium build, can be modified to cover this variable.

A fine boned horse can be given 2 lbs less than the total calculated and a heavy horse will need 2 lbs more. For example a 16 hand thoroughbred will need 28 lbs and a heavy hunter type of the same height, 32 lbs.

Grass Kept Horses and Ponies

The amounts as calculated are for fully stabled horses and ponies and for those allowed very little pasture time. Horses and ponies living out at grass during the winter will also need the *same amount of food as a stabled horse*. They need this to maintain their health and condition during wet or cold weather.

For horses and ponies kept at grass from early spring right through to autumn before the weather becomes cold and the grass loses its goodness, the amount of supplementary foods can be reduced. Native ponies living at grass during the warmer months with a light or medium workload will need very little extra food.

At Stage I level candidates are not expected to know the variations for feeding animals kept at grass, it is sufficient to understand that the amount of supplementary foods needed will vary during the seasons.

Percentages

The next element is the percentage of concentrates to roughage that the horse will need. This depends on the amount and type of work that the horse is expected to perform. A horse in light work certainly does not need a lot of energy giving food. This would 'heat him up' and make him unmanageable. Conversely a horse in hard work needs the extra 'hard' or concentrated food to enable him to perform safely, satisfactorily and to keep him healthy.

The amount of concentrates and roughage is calculated basically from the hours of work.

Level of Work	Hours of work	Type of work	Percentages
Light Work	Approximately 4 - 6 hours a week.	Hacking, light schooling, some riding school horses and most ponies.	30% concentrates to 70% bulk.
Medium Work	Approximately 6 to 10 hours a week.	Schooling up to 2 hours a day, dressage, show jumping and hacking.	50% concentrates to 50% bulk.
Hard work	10 hours and over or hard, fast work.	Eventing, hunting, point to point, racing, endurance riding.	70% concentrates to 30% bulk.

For Example; a 16 hand Irish Draught/Thoroughbred, medium build, doing 10 hours schooling and hacking a week will need a total daily amount of 30 lbs. This will be split 50/50 with 15 lbs of concentrate and 15 lbs of roughage.

There is one important point that must be considered; *all horses are individuals*. The calculated amount, whilst being a good basic beginning, may need varying if necessary.

The horse should be monitored over a period of time to see that the amount suits him. If he puts on weight or becomes a little 'hot', the concentrates ration may be reduced and the roughage increased. If he loses weight or condition then his feed may need altering as necessary.

Having calculated a daily amount, this is then split into three or four feeds a day. The concentrate ration is given as one in the morning, one in the evening and one or two during the day depending on the horse's timetable. Keeping in mind that no one feed should be more than 5 or 6 lbs, the largest feed can be given at night and at breakfast, providing the horse is not being worked too early. For example our horse is fed 15 lbs of hard feed he can have; 4 lbs in the morning, 3 lbs at midday, 3 lbs for tea and 5 lbs at night. The hay ration can be divided in the same way; the largest portion given with the last feed at night.

Exam Tip

For the examination you will need to learn thoroughly the aims, rules and considerations of feeding. You must also try to *understand* them and the reasons why they are important. You should be able to calculate the daily amount of food by height and the percentage of hard and bulk foods from the amount of work the horse is doing.

Feeding is the 'pet' subject of quite a few examiners who may probe deeply into this aspect of horse care. You are not expected to be an expert on feeding nor to be able to conjure the accurate amounts out of your head immediately. Do not be confused if the examiner suddenly throws a question at you as follows:

How much hard food would a 15 hand Welsh cob/Thoroughbred need per day doing about 10 hours a week at a riding school?

Take one step at a time:

1. **Height** ⇨ **amount**
    Work out how much food in total from height = 26 lbs.

2. **Build** ⇨ **amount**
    Consider build, cob/thoroughbred should be medium = 26 lbs.

3. **Work** ⇨ **percentages**
    Decide what type of work = medium
    What percentage of hard food is needed = 50%.
    50% of 26 lbs is 13 lbs of hard food per day.

Always state that this is the initial amount to feed this horse but *he should be monitored for a few weeks or months to see if this suits him.*

Feeding horses is a complex, complicated and often confusing subject, particularly as it depends on so many variables, traditions and personal preferences. Learning the basics step by step; understanding the reasons, rules and considerations will certainly help to illuminate the mystique of feeding.

C H A P T E R   13
Types of Feed

Grass is the natural diet of the horse and the *right pasture* at *certain seasons* of the year, provides all the nutrients in the right quantities for his maintenance. *Maintenance is defined as that level at which a horse can be kept in good condition without doing any work, or in some cases performing light work.* Once the horse is asked to work longer hours or more strenuous exercise he will need extra foods and different types to maintain his condition.

Basically, food is divided into two categories:

1.   Concentrates

These provide the horse with energy and maintain his condition; grains and cereals such as oats, barley and maize. This also covers foods that are added to provide extra nutrients and to make the feed more tasty; such as molasses and linseed. (These are termed 'openers' or 'mixers'.)

Into this category as well fit the specifically manufactured 'Compound' feeds. These are made up by Feed Companies and sold as hard cubes, nuts and wafers or as a mix.

2.   Roughage

This adds bulk to the diet and slows down the rate at which the concentrates pass through the digestive system giving time for the nutrients to be absorbed; foods such as hay and chaff (chopped hay or straw). Some traditional foods, such as Bran, and openers such as Sugar Beet, are also used for their bulk content to add roughage to the diet.

Traditional Feeds

Because the domesticated horse has an artificial lifestyle, he needs extra foods to make up for the lack of pasture and to provide the extra energy needed for the work performed. Over the centuries various foodstuffs have been used for equine nutrition and these have become known as Traditional feeds.

Oats

❖ This grain is considered the best as it is the closest nutritionally to the horse's needs.

❖ It is high in energy yet does not make the horse fat.

❖ Good quality oats are hard, clean, plump, heavy, golden and sweet smelling.

❖ Oats are best fed either bruised, rolled, crushed or crimped.

▲ Oats lack certain minerals and should be fed with the addition of other foods.

▲ Oats should never be fed in excess as this can make the horse 'hot' and uncontrollable.

▲ Bad quality oats are thin, dark in colour and smell sour and should not be used for feed.

▲ Once the husk has been broken open, the oats start to lose their value and should not be kept longer than 3 weeks.

▲ Whilst whole oats are often fed quite successfully, some horses may have difficulty digesting them.

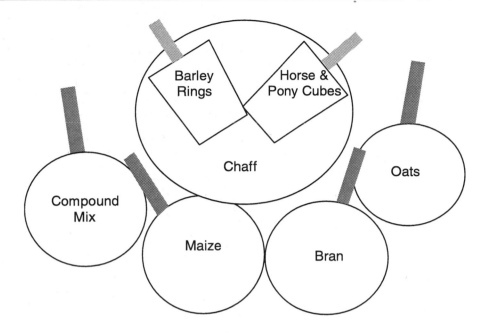

Barley

❖ Barley has almost the same nutritional value and can be fed as a substitute for oats.

❖ It is slightly less heating but more fattening, therefore good for a horse who needs to put on weight.

❖ Barley can be fed flaked, rolled, crushed, boiled, or micronized.

  ▲ This cereal needs to be fed with other food because of the low fibre content and lack of certain minerals.

  ▲ It is low in fibre.

  ▲ The grains are small, hard, difficult to chew and therefore must not be fed whole unless cooked.

Maize

❖ Maize provides extra energy and is beneficial for horses in hard work.

❖ The high starch content puts weight on a thin animal.

❖ Maize is normally fed flaked or micronized, is yellow and similar in appearance to corn flakes.

  ▲ The protein content is of low quality.

  ▲ Fibre content too is very low.

  ▲ Maize is very heating and should be fed in small amounts of no more than 25% (one quarter) of the total grain fed.

Bran

Bran is made from the husks of wheat grain separated from the flour. It is a roughage food, with the appearance of fine brown bread crumbs.

❖   Bran adds extra bulk to the diet.

❖   A bran mash can be fed to a horse who is off work and box resting, as a laxative.

❖   A bran mash is also beneficial for a tired horse after long, hard work or as a feed on the night before the horse's rest day.

❖   Bran helps to alleviate minor bowel conditions. For instance dry bran can be given to a horse with loose droppings, (diarrhoea). As a laxative to help in cases of mild constipation, bran can be fed wet as in a mash.

❖   Bran can be useful as a medium for administering medicines.

Though bran used to be considered an essential part of the horse's diet, it is unpopular nowadays for two reasons.

1.   With the efficiency of the milling process of flour it is difficult to purchase good quality bran.

2.   It is considered to be nutritionally incorrect. Amongst the elements contained within Bran are the two minerals Calcium and Phosphorus. These need to be present in the diet at the correct ratio; approximately two parts calcium to one part phosphorus. However, bran contains a high level of phosphorus and a low level of calcium which, if fed exclusively and excessively, creates an imbalance in the diet. Calcium is essential for bone development and a deficiency of this mineral can cause bone deformities and weaknesses. This is particularly so in young animals who can developed rickets.

For these reasons many establishments will not feed bran at all. Some yards and stables feed bran with the addition of limestone flour to make up for the deficiency of calcium.

Linseed

Linseed is the seed of the flax plant. In appearance the uncooked seeds are small, oval, shiny and brown.

❖ Linseed is high in protein, fats and oils.

❖ It is traditionally fed to horses in winter or in poor condition as a pick-me-up.

❖ It improves the condition of the horse's coat giving it a shine and gloss.

❖ It can also improve hoof condition.

❖ Depending on the amount of water added Linseed can either be fed as a jelly or a tea.

❖ Linseed oil can be purchased in bottles similar to normal vegetable oil. This, of course, saves a lot of time.

▲ It is **very poisonous** if not prepared properly.

▲ Linseed should always be fed sparingly, no more than 3 to 4 ozs of dried seed three times a week.

Peas/Beans

❖ Peas/Beans are rich in protein.

❖ They are fed split or crushed to horses in hard work.

❖ These legumes provide energy and help to maintain weight.

▲ Fed in excess peas and beans are heating and fattening, no more than about 1 lb should be added to any one feed.

Molasses

Molasses is a by-product from the production of sugar; in appearance a dark, sticky syrup that looks like black treacle.

❖ It supplies energy and improves the condition of the coat.

❖ Small quantities only are needed and one teaspoon in warm water poured over the food is sufficient.

❖ Most commercial compound feeds include molasses in their ingredients.

❖ It has a very sweet taste which tempts poor feeders or fussy eaters.

▲ Its palatability should not be used to encourage a horse to eat poor quality or stale food.

Sugar Beet

❖ Sugar Beet is a good source of energy and roughage.

❖ It is beneficial to horses doing longer, slower work as in riding schools or hacking.

❖ Sugar beet maintains weight and also, being a roughage food, adds bulk to the diet.

▲ Because it is relatively slow to digest, the bulk in the gut makes it an unsuitable food for horses doing fast work.

▲ Sugar beet comes in the form of shreds or cubes, both of which must be soaked thoroughly before being fed. If eaten dry, sugar beet will swell in the horse's stomach causing severe colic or even death. Sugar beet shreds are soaked in a double amount of water for 12 hours. The cubes need soaking in a triple amount of water for 24 hours.

▲ Cold water must always be used for the soaking. Though the beet does ferment even in cold water, hot water will make it ferment much more quickly.

▲ The pulp must also be kept cool, particularly on hot days, and fed within a few hours.

▲ Sugar beet needs feeding in small amounts, no more than 3 lbs soaked weight each day.

▲ It does have a laxative effect on some horses.

Sugar beet cubes look very similar to horse and pony cubes. When stored they must be clearly labelled so that they are not fed by mistake. This could be fatal to a horse or pony.

Soyabean Meal

❖ Soyabean meal is extremely high in protein.

❖ An excellent addition to the feed for horses in hard work.

  ▲ It should be fed sparingly, no more than 1 lb per day, as an excessive amount of protein can cause digestive problems.

Salt

❖ Salt is an essential part of the horse's diet. The chemical reactions that take place within the body actually occur in a salt solution.

❖ This mineral is provided as a salt lick or as rock salt in the manager.

❖ Blocks can be bought either unflavoured or with the addition of minerals or mint.

❖ Another method is to add one to four ounces to the feed each day.

❖ Salt is particularly important in the summer when horses are working hard. Water and salts are lost through sweating.

Compound Feeds

Over the past decade or so Feed Merchants have found equine nutrition commercially viable. Many manufacturers now employ professional nutritionists who research into a variety of foodstuffs for horses. The trend now is towards a food that is a complete and balanced mix of all the nutrients necessary to the horse. The great advantage of Compound food is that they are very simple to use. Instead of having to weigh and mix a variety of traditional feeds there is just one food to give very easily and quickly.

These 'compound foods' are split into two types-

1. **Nuts, cubes or wafers** - the ingredients are ground up, steamed and pelleted.

2. **'Coarse mix'** - appears more as a traditional feed.

There are various types of compound food. These are made up for horses and ponies of all ages, in all types of work and environment, even those who are ill and resting. For example; there are Competition Cubes or Performances Mixes for those horses in hard work and competing. Stud Cubes or Yearling Cubes are available for brood mares and foals. Convalescence Mixes or Cereal Meals are specifically for invalid horses out of work. Leaflets listing all the different types are available from local Feed Merchants.

Manufacturers use many different names for similar foods but there is no difference between one type of cube and its corresponding mix. For instance; a competition cube will have just the same nutritional value as a competition mix. The choice is based on the preference of the horse or owner.

Advantages of compound foods:

❖ Provides a constant, balanced diet.

❖ Easy to feed, especially when different members of staff make up the feeds.

❖ Easy to store, one bag of compound food instead of three or so bags of traditional foods.

❖ Easy to transport.

❖ Labour saving.

❖ Clean.

❖ Dust free.

❖ Palatable. Most of the compound foods include molasses.

❖ Always of good quality. Manufacturers keen to keep their good reputation make sure they buy the best foodstuffs, so the quality is guaranteed.

❖ Time saving, no mixing or weighing three of four different foods.

❖ Take away the 'guesswork' by providing one food for any type of horse.

Disadvantages of compound foods:

▲ Expensive unless ordered in bulk.

▲ The cubes or nuts, unless moistened or dampened, can be dry - risk of choking.

▲ Not easy to adjust. With a traditional food, such as oats, it is simple to increase the amount in the feed. With compound foods, (though it is possible to mix one sort of compound feed with another), a whole new bag would have to be bought to give the horse a different balance. This is awkward for large establishments that buy in bulk.

▲ They may be boring as a diet. This relates to the cubes or nuts; the mix certainly seems appetising. In any case it is hard to believe that an animal whose natural food is grass could find compound foods boring. Some horses may refuse to eat cubes or nuts but this is generally due to some ingredient in the cube.

▲ This food deteriorates when stored. This is true but so does all other foods when kept for any length of time.

Chaff, Mollichop (chaff with molasses) and sugar beet are often mixed in with a compound food but, according to the Manufacturers, it is inadvisable to add anything else such as oats or barley. This will cause an nutritional imbalance. All compound foods, except for those produced as mixers or supplements, are designed to be a complete meal including all the nutrients necessary.

Compound foods are extremely popular; most owners, grooms and stables feed these nowadays. They are a simple, balanced, complete diet that eliminates the labour-intensive and time-consuming part of making up traditional foods.

Cooked Foods

Some foods such as linseed must be cooked. For oats and barley steaming or boiling softens the grain and makes them easier to digest. Steaming is preferable; during boiling some nutrients are dissolved in the water and lost from the food.

Aged horses who have trouble chewing and digesting, invalid horses, tired or overworked horses or shy eaters can all be fed cooked foods. As can those who get little or no time at grass, in which case cooking their food can help to prevent constipation.

Oats

Ingredients.

- 2 to 4 lbs oats or quantity as required.

- Water; at a ratio of one part oats - two parts water.

- A teaspoonful of salt.

Method.

Boiled: Place the oats and water in a pan and bring to the boil. Continue boiling until the oats are soft. The mixture must be watched carefully in case it starts to burn. Add salt and leave until cool enough to eat.

(When boiled oats tend to absorb a lot of water. This can give the horse a fat, soft condition.)

Steamed: Put the oats into a large sieve and place this over the water in a pan. Cover the pan and boil the water gently until the oats are soft.

Cooked oats can be mixed with boiled barley, bran mash or other cooked foods.

Barley

Ingredients

- 2 to 3 lbs of Barley or amount required.
- Water; ratio of one part barley and two parts water.
- A teaspoonful of salt.

Method

Boiled   Whole barley is boiled in a similar fashion to oats then allowed to simmer for 4 to 6 hours until the grains split and soften.

Mash   To make a mash use flaked barley. Place the barley into a bucket and pour on boiling water. Cover and leave until cool then add the salt. A barley mash can be fed to a horse after hard exercise, to fussy eaters and those that are underweight.

Cooked barley may also be mixed with cooked bran or oats.

Bran mash

Ingredients

- 2 to 4 lbs bran or 2/3 of a bucket.
- Up to 1/3 of a bucket of boiling water.
- 2 ozs limestone flour.

Method

Pour some of the boiling water onto the bran in the bucket. Stir and add more water if required. The bran should be damp and crumbly but *not too wet*. Cover and leave until cool enough to eat. To test for the right consistency, take a handful of bran when cool enough and squeeze it into a ball. This should hold its shape. Add limestone flour and linseed jelly, oats or boiled barley and salt if required.

Linseed Jelly

Ingredients

- 2 to 3 ozs dried seed.
- 4 pints of water.

Method.

Cover the linseed with water and soak overnight. Then add the rest of the water to the linseed mixture and bring to the boil. Watch the linseed carefully as it can burn or boil over, if necessary add more water. Simmer for six hours and allow to cool. This will solidify into a jelly. Add linseed jelly to bran mash or other foods. To make linseed tea simply add more water. Linseed must be properly cooked otherwise it is *very poisonous*. It can be cooked with other foods such as oats or barley, as long as the seeds are cooked thoroughly enough.

Oatmeal Gruel

Ingredients

- 2 handfuls of oatmeal.
- Boiling water.

Method

Place the oatmeal into a bucket and pour on boiling water until the mixture is the right consistency; either crumbly or wet enough to drink. Stir well and allow to cool. This gruel is particularly beneficial for an ill horse or one that has difficulty eating.

Some cooked foods can take quite a long time to prepare. Stables or yards who frequently feed cooked foods purchase slow cookers or Oat Boilers.

Exam Tip

During the session on feeding you will be handed, or asked to choose, a sample of food. You will then be questioned about the sample; asked to name it, describe it, to give its properties, advantages and disadvantages. You will also be asked to assess the quality. The examiner may probe further and ask when each type of food should be fed to a horse and in what quantity. There may be a general group discussion about the advantages of feeding traditional or compound feed and the reasons for these preferences.

Before the exam you will need to familiarise yourself with different foodstuffs and compare good and bad quality feed. Take particular notice of sugar beet cubes, make sure you know the difference between these and pony cubes.

A visit to the local feed merchant is useful; to look at the different feeds available. There are usually leaflets and booklets which you can take home and study at your leisure.

Do not, however, overload yourself with too much information. There is a bewildering selection of feeds and supplements which can be confusing. Learning about the basic feeds and their properties as well as having an awareness of the varieties available, is quite sufficient for the Stage I.

C H A P T E R   14
Hay and Haynets

Roughage is a vital part of the diet and should make up *at least 30% of the total daily food intake*. Hay, which is basically dried, cut grass, is mostly composed of fibre and provides the majority of roughage in the diet for stabled horses. It is the essential foundation of a good diet for horses living in all year round and for grass kept horses during autumn, winter and early spring. All hay should be of good quality; inferior hay should never be fed to horses or ponies.

Types of Hay

There are two types of hay, Seed hay and Meadow hay.

1.   **Seed hay**

- The grasses for this type of hay are sown as an annual crop and contain top quality plants such as rye grass.
- Seed hay is nutritious, suitable for horses in hard work.
- This hay is usually free of weeds and poisonous plants.
- It is tougher than meadow hay and more difficult to digest.
- It is more expensive than meadow hay.
- It should be stored for at least six months to one year before use. New hay can cause digestive problems such as diarrhoea.

2.   **Meadow hay**

- This type of hay is cut from natural pasture.
- The grasses are allowed to grow naturally, which means meadow hay usually contains a greater variety of plants.
- It may also contain some inferior grasses.
- The grass is allowed to go to seed before cutting. This gives a softer and sweeter hay, considered by some to be more palatable for the horse.
- This hay is suitable for all horses.
- It is less expensive than seed hay.
- It should be stored for about six months before being fed.
- Meadow hay is often greener than seed hay.

Hay Quality

All hay should be of good quality and it is important to be able to recognise good hay and to distinguish it from inferior grades.

	Good quality hay	*Inferior Hay.*
Smell	Clean, sweet, pleasant smell.	Sour, tangy, musty, damp and mouldy.
Colour	Varying from green-brown to golden-brown.	Colourless or dark brown to black. Watch out for hay that has white areas and black areas. This is 'mow-burnt' hay that has overheated in the rick; caused by baling before the stems are dry.
		Very green - the hay is too new to feed, and will cause digestive problems.
Feel	Dry and crisp.	Wet, damp, slimy, dusty.
Dust	It will be as free of dust as possible.	Dusty and powdery.
Content	Good quality grasses with no poisonous plants.	Inferior grasses, quantities of weeds and poisonous plants.
Taste (try the other tests first!)	Sweet and chewy.	Sour, musty and bitter.

To test the quality of hay; check the bale for colour, particularly at the edges where it may be mouldy, wet or black. Take some hay and smell it, check for texture and look for any poisonous plants or weeds.

The quality of hay depends on many variables such as; the **types of grasses** from which it is made, the **land and soil** on which it is grown, the farmer and his **standard of grassland management**, the **time of year** it is cut, **weather conditions** and how it is **stored**. Hay quality can vary from year to year depending on the weather.

Other Types of Forage

There are other methods of conserving grass which to some extent limit these variables. Their differences are dependant on the moisture quantity and the method of packaging.

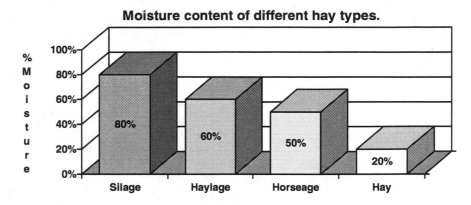

Moisture content of different hay types.

Vacuum-Packed Forage (usually known as HorseHage*)

HorseHage* is hay in a different form. (There are several different spellings of this name but they all refer to the same vacuum-packed semi-wilted grass.)

It is produced to combat the respiratory problems in horses caused by dust and fungal spores. It is completely dust free.

HorseHage is made up of the best quality grasses, usually ryegrass or alfalfa mixtures. It is always of a good quality unlike normal hay that can vary.

The grass is cut and baled within a matter of days so that it only partially dries. In comparison to hay which is 80% dry, HorseHage is around 50% dry. The bales are compressed to half their size, then vacuum-packed and sealed to exclude air.

Fermentation takes place within the bale. This preserves the nutrient levels within the grass. It also gives HorseHage its rich golden colour, sweet smell and taste. Most horses love it.

HorseHage can either be fed straight away or, because it is vacuum-packed, kept up to a year or more. Once a bale is opened however, (even if accidentally torn), the HorseHage will deteriorate if not used within 5 days.

Though HorseHage provides the bulk in the diet, it is far more nutritious than normal hay and therefore is fed in smaller quantities. Even the concentrate quota may be reduced slightly except for horses in really hard work.

---

* HorseHage is the registered name of Marksway HorseHage.

It is excellent for fussy eaters, those doing faster work and, because it is dust free, for those with respiratory problems.

It is however more expensive than ordinary hay, usually about twice the price.

There are approximately five types of HorseHage on the market at present, but the two main ones are the Ryegrass or high protein HorseHage and low protein/high fibre HorseHage.

Haylage.

This is often confused with HorseHage, but it is different. Haylage is very similar to Silage but with a lower moisture content; being approximately 40% dry. Sometimes haylage is fed to horses but it is not as popular as HorseHage. It usually comes in big bales that are not very easy to store, handle or transport.

Silage

This is not a popular feed for horses as deaths from Botulism after eating silage have been recorded, some very recently. However, a few establishments are experimenting with types of silage and may be feeding it with some success.

Silage is wilted grass, 25% dry, treated and sealed in large, airtight bags. Some silage includes additives that may not be suitable for horses.

How to Feed Hay

Hay can either be fed dry, moistened or wet. Whilst in most cases good quality hay may be fed dry quite satisfactorily, there are a number of horses and ponies who develop problems when given dry hay. Hay contains fungal spores which, when inhaled through the nostrils, can cause an allergic reaction. This may develop into ailments ranging from a simple cough with a discharge from the nostrils, to respiratory problems and damage to the lungs. In this case the hay should be dampened; some yards prefer to damp down all the hay.

When the hay is moistened, by soaking in water or steaming, the fungal spores swell so that they become too large to pass into the lungs. Also when wet, the spores tend to stick to the stems in the hay instead of being inhaled.

Soaking

Hay can be soaked for several hours or even overnight. However, some of the water-soluble nutrients are washed out of the hay and drain away with the excess water. Also, if left submerged for a long time, hay begins to smell sour and some horses refuse to eat it.

It is now considered that 20 minutes is sufficient. Tests have shown that this is ample time for soaking and fewer of the nutrients are lost.

Method

The hay is put into a haynet, placed into a container such as a plastic dustbin and water is poured over it from a hosepipe. Some yards have water tanks into which the whole bale is immersed.

Steaming

This is preferable as the nutrient loss is minimized. The haynet is placed in a rubber or plastic dustbin or tank, and boiling water is poured over it. The container is covered and the hay left to cool.

Haynets

There are different ways in which hay can be fed to horses in the stable or out in the field. Certainly in the box the most economical, convenient and hygienic method is from a haynet.

Haynets are available in a variety of sizes, colours and materials; from plain brown rope nets to brightly coloured nylon, with large or small holes. The decision as to which type to purchase depends on the type of hay fed and the personal preference of the owner. Nets with smaller holes can be used to feed HorseHage as this makes the smaller proportions last longer.

Feeding hay in a net does have certain advantages over other methods:

* It is easier to weigh the hay, giving a more accurate calculation of feed.

* It is less wasteful than feeding hay off the floor and though the horse does drop some hay onto the ground this tends to stay clean and can be put back into the net.

* Haynets are easier to carry.

* It is convenient when travelling. Haynets can be used in trailers, horse boxes, or outside on a fence.

* The haynet can be used at varying heights to suit a horse or a pony.

* It is more hygienic, as it keeps hay off the floor yet does not allow spores or dust into the horse's eyes.

* Birds and vermin cannot live in it.

* Damping down or steaming hay is much more efficiently done in a haynet.

Haynets do have some disadvantages:

- The net can be heavy when the hay is wet. (Though wet hay is heavy whatever method is used.)

- If not correctly tied up, the net may become tangled around the horse's legs causing injury.

- Haynets can be damaged and need repairing or replacing.

How To Fill, Weigh And Tie Up

To fill a haynet

Gently shake and loosen a wedge or two of hay. Hold the net by the top and open the neck as wide as possible. If convenient, ask someone to hold the neck open while the hay is placed inside. Once the correct amount has been placed in the net, tighten the string.

Weighing

Weighing the haynet is relatively easy with the use of hanging scales. The scales are suspended from a nail or hook in a convenient spot and the haynet placed on the weighing hook.

Tying up a Haynet

The important point about tying up a haynet is to raise it *high enough, so that when empty the net does not hang too low.* If the empty net drops low enough there is a risk that the horse will trap a leg in the net either when rolling or pawing the stable wall.

The securing ring onto which the haynet is tied, should be about five feet above the level of the bed.

Pull the drawstring through the ring
as far as possible.

Keep the net steady, by holding it with a hand or
placing a knee beneath it, and place the end of the string
through the lower part of the net.

Pull the string and draw the net up as high as possible,
securing it with a quick release knot.

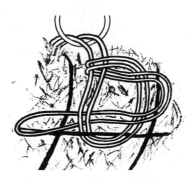

Twist the net around so that the knot is against the
wall, preventing the horse from pulling the knot too
tight or releasing the net.

The net must always be tied with a quick release
knot then, if the horse does manage to become
caught up, it can be unfastened quickly.

In the field a haynet must always be tied up safely; at a correct height with a quick
release knot for exactly the same reason as in the stable.

Other Feeding Methods

There are other ways in which to feed hay to a horse and briefly these are:

Hayracks

In the box

A hayrack, usually made of metal bars placed high in a corner of the box, saves time as the hay can simply be placed into the rack. Racks are not used as much these days as there are certain disadvantages:

- They tend to be positioned rather high up, making it quite difficult to put the hay in.

- It is unnatural for a horse to feed in this position.

- The height allows dust and spores to fall into the horse's eyes and nostrils when eating.

- Old hay often gets left inside and goes mouldy.

- Birds and vermin often use this as a nest.

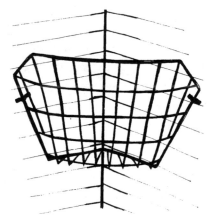 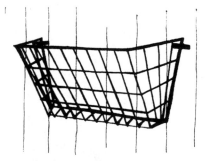

In the field

Here the hayrack is the most economical and efficient method of feeding hay. There are no problems providing the rack is **appropriately situated** in the field so that the **ground does not become poached.** It must also be a **horse feeding rack;** not a cow rack.

- The only disadvantage is that if one of the horses in the herd is a bully, he may prevent other horses feeding from the rack.

The Floor

In the box

Some yards prefer this method as it is **convenient, labour saving** and **more natural for the horse** to eat from the ground. It does have certain disadvantages:

- It causes a **lot of waste**. The horse mixes the hay up with the bedding and can stale on it.

- It may **encourage bed eating.**

- There is an increased possibility of **infestation by worms** as larvae from droppings can migrate to the food on the floor and be ingested.

In the field

This is certainly safer than haynets or hayracks, with the horses and ponies eating the hay quite simply off the ground. It can help to minimize fighting and bullying; several piles of hay can be placed separately from each other, allowing those horses further down the pecking order a chance of getting enough fodder.

- This method is wasteful, as the hay is kicked around the field, trampled on and left uneaten.

Exam Tip

In this section you may be asked to name the different types of hay and to recognise good and bad quality. You will also be asked to describe the various methods of feeding hay and how to fill and tie up a haynet. If there is a net available, one of the candidates will be asked to tie this up.

As part of the preparation for the exam, take a look at some hay, test its quality by appearance, feel and smell; compare this with HorseHage. Practise filling and tying up a haynet correctly, so that you gain practical experience and will not be worried if asked to do this in the exam.

CHAPTER 15
Snaffle Bridle

A bridle is used to control the horse's pace, speed and direction. There are several different designs of bridles and bits that assist in achieving this control, such as the snaffle, pelham, kimblewick, the gag, the double and the bitless bridle. For the Stage I candidates need to know about the snaffle bridle; the various bits in the snaffle group and the different nosebands used in conjunction with this bridle.

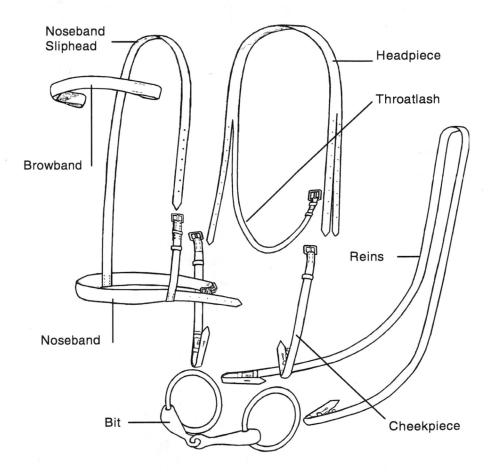

Figure 45: Points of the Snaffle Bridle.

Parts of the Bridle

A snaffle bridle consists of the bit, cheekpieces, headpiece, noseband and sliphead, throatlash, reins and browband.

Reins

The longest reins measure 5 feet, used mainly for show jumping or eventing. Normally reins measure 4 feet 6 inches with pony reins measuring 4 feet 3 inches. It is important that reins are of the **correct length**.

Reins that are too short will encourage the rider to lean forward in an incorrect position. Long reins are dangerous as they can become caught around the rider's foot and stirrup. This is particularly so for children on ponies

Reins are made from different materials depending on use or personal preference. Leather is the most popular and is available in plain, plaited or laced designs. Leather reins can also be covered with rubber. Other materials include webbing, nylon and linen.

Reins of plaited leather or those covered with rubber are more practical, particularly for jumping, eventing or in wet weather. These provide a firmer hold and help to prevent the reins from slipping through the fingers.

Browband

The browband is the part that fits around the front of the head, just below the ears. It is connected by loops to the headpiece and prevents the bridle from slipping backwards down the horse's neck.

Browbands are available either as plain leather or decorated with brass studs or fancy stitching. They can also be purchased wrapped in velvet ribbon in a variety of colours.

If the browband is too small it will cause discomfort and rubbing around the ears. Too large and it will flap or allow the bridle to slip backwards.

Headpiece

The headpiece, which fits over the head behind the ears, includes the throatlash and the straps to which the cheekpieces fasten.

When the cheekpieces are connected to the straps of the headpiece, the buckles should lie above the horse's eyes under the browband. Any lower would indicate that the bridle is too large or the cheekpieces too small. The buckles might also catch and damage the eye. The cheekpieces on both sides should also be of equal length so that the bit is level in the mouth.

Throatlash

The throatlash or throatlatch fits under the cheek and around the throat of the horse. This prevents the bridle coming off if, for some reason, it is pulled forwards.

Correct fitting should allow the horse to flex his neck without any restriction to his breathing. The handler should be able to get the *width of a hand* between the cheekbone and the throatlash.

The throatlash is fastened on the nearside of the horse's head.

The Bit

The bit is connected to the cheekpieces. If the cheekpieces are correctly fitted to the headpiece then the bit should be level in the mouth.

Mouthpieces are made from a variety of materials; stainless steel, chromium plated steel, pure nickel, copper, vulcanite, nylon, rubber and the more recent Nathe bit. This has a metal strip covered with a pale yellow, rubbery plastic.

Stainless steel is the strongest and the best.

Nickel	Recognised by its yellow appearance, Nickel is not used extensively because it is weak and tends to snap.
Vulcanite	Is rubber made stronger by heat treatment.
Rubber	Is kind to the horse's mouth but, because of its softness, can be bitten through.

Types of Snaffle Mouthpiece

There are three main types of snaffle mouthpiece:

Single Jointed

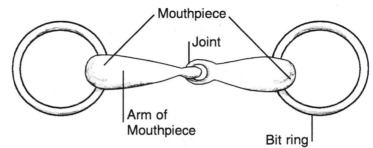

This bit has a single joint in centre of the mouthpiece. Bits with thick arms are generally milder than thin armed bits though it can depend on the size of the horse's mouth. A horse with a small mouth can find a thick bit uncomfortable. *The single jointed snaffle has a 'nutcracker' action.*

Double Jointed

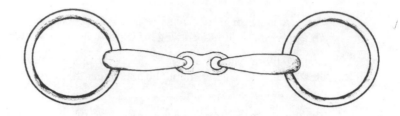

These bits have a link in the centre of the bit. The **French Link** is considered by some to be milder than the single jointed snaffle as it has no nutcracker action. The link lies flat on the tongue. The **Dr. Bristol**, on the other hand, is a very severe bit because of the angle of the link, which puts more pressure on the tongue.

Straight Bar and Mullen Mouth

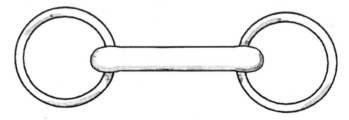

These have no joints and are the mildest form of bit. The **Mullen Mouth** has a slight half moon shape allowing more room for the tongue. These bits are often made from Vulcanite, or metal covered with rubber.

Ring Types

There are also a variety of rings that connect the bit to the bridle. The most popular are:

Loose Ring

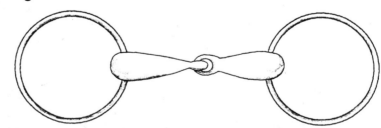

The loose ring snaffle has large rings that pass through holes at the end of the mouthpiece.

★   Because the bit moves more easily on the rings, it allows the smallest movement of the hands to be transmitted to the horse's mouth.

★ The loose ring allows the horse to 'mouth' or play with the bit without interference from the rider's hands.

★ A Loose or wire ring is useful on a young horse because it is more difficult for these rings to be pulled through an open mouth.

▲ Where the ring passes through the mouthpiece the metal can wear thin and become very sharp, sometimes cutting the horse's lips.

Eggbutt

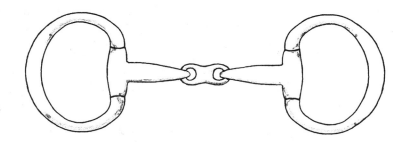

The mouthpiece is rounded and tapered onto the rings in the shape of a 'T'.

★ This type of ring, because of its shape, does not wear thin and eliminates the problem of cutting and pinching at the corner of the mouth.

▲ The eggbut is much less mobile and not suitable for a horse with a dry mouth or a fixed jaw.

▲ Because this design does not allow any movement between the ring and the mouthpiece, the bit itself can become more 'fixed' within the mouth, particularly if the rider is a novice or has strong hands.

D Ring

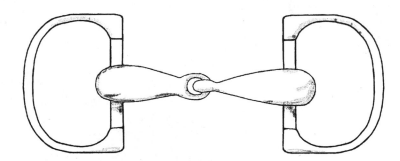

Named because the ring looks like a D.

★ Prevents the ring from being pulled through the mouth.

Bit Variations

The following are variations of the bit itself rather than the ring:

Loose Ringed Fulmer

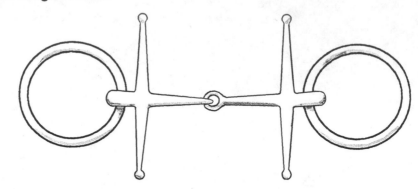

This bit has long cheekpieces. It is usually known as the 'Fulmer' or the 'Australian Loose ringed snaffle'. The cheekpieces should be fitted into keepers attached to the bridle to hold the bit in place.

★   Good for young horses or those that open the mouth as the cheekpieces prevent the bit from being pulled through.

★   The 'cheeks' help to steer the horse by pressing on the opposite side of the mouth.

★   This is considered to be suitable for riding school horses as it lessens the effect of novice hands on the horse's mouth.

▲   Some horses learn to evade this bit by 'leaning' on the long cheek pieces.

Full Cheek Snaffle

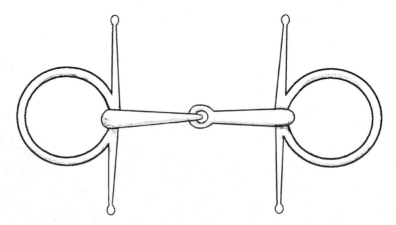

This is similar to the Loose Ringed Fulmer except the cheekpieces are part of the ring.

★   Good for young horses as in the Fulmer.

▲   This bit can tend to have a more fixed and less mobile action.

There are other sorts of snaffle that have cheek pieces but the above two are the most popular.

Nosebands

There are types of noseband which, being fitted at varying heights on the horse's face, have different functions. The sliphead is the slim strap placed under the headpiece and through the loops of the browband to connect the noseband to the bridle.

Cavesson Noseband

This is the commonest type in use and consists of a plain noseband and sliphead. Usually made of leather, it fits around the horse's face below the cheekbones.

Its use is mainly cosmetic, giving the horse's face a better appearance by foreshortening the length. It is also used in conjunction with the standing martingale, almost the only noseband to do so apart from the Flash.

Fit

When fitted correctly the noseband should lie *two fingers width* below the projecting cheek bone and have *two fingers width* between it and the horse's face. This is checked by placing two fingers between the nose band and the horse's nasal bone on the front of his face.

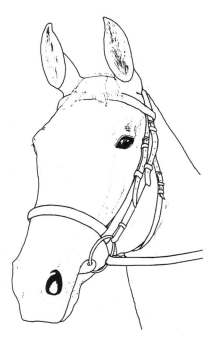

Figure 46: Cavesson Noseband.

Flash

This is a cavesson noseband with a loop attached at the centre through which a thin strap is passed - *the flash strap*. This strap goes *below* the bit, round into the chin groove. Both the cavesson part and the flash strap are fastened firmly. This is to prevent the horse evading the bit by crossing its jaw or opening its mouth.

The flash was originally designed to combine the properties of the cavesson and drop noseband. A standing martingale could theoretically be attached to the top portion.

Fit

The cavesson part is placed in the same position as the normal cavesson but fastened slightly tighter. The flash strap must be four fingers width above the nostril to prevent restricting the horse's breathing. The tightness of the flash must allow room for one finger to fit underneath. Its purpose is to prevent the horse from opening his mouth. The buckle should **not** be fastened in the chin groove or around the lips in case it injures the horse.

Figure 47: Flash Noseband.

Drop noseband

The front portion, between the sliphead straps, is similar to a narrow cavesson and fits over the front of the nose. The lower straps, those to the back, are connected by rings to the sliphead, pass below the bit and into the chin groove.

Fit

The frontal strap should not be fastened too low. There should be *four fingers width* above the nostrils.

The Drop straps should be fastened *tightly enough* to prevent evasion, but not so tightly as to clamp the mouth shut or impede breathing. There should be enough room for one finger's width between the drop strap and the horse's face. The buckle ideally should not be fastened in the chin groove or interfere with the lips.

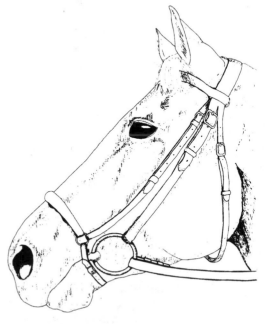

Figure 48: Drop Noseband.

Grakle

This consists of two straps of leather crossing over the front of the nose. There should be a small leather pad lined with sheepskin where the straps cross to prevent chafing on the horse's face.

The Grakle prevents the horse opening his mouth or crossing the jaw but, in acting over a larger area of the head and the pressure point on the nose, it has a stronger effect.

Fit

The top straps are connected to the sliphead and fasten behind the jaw. The position of these straps is slightly higher than a cavesson, just below the protruding cheek bone. The lower straps fit below the bit and in the chin groove, similar to the flash.

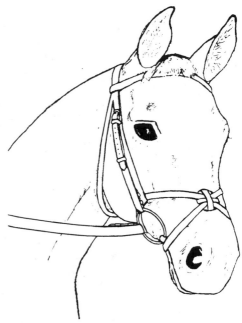

Figure 49: Grakle Noseband.

Sheepskin Noseband

This covers a cavesson and its purpose is to keep the horse's attention from straying by focusing it forward. This is used mainly for racehorses.

These are the nosebands in normal use. A snaffle bridle can be used without a noseband but this tends to make the horse's face look long.

Putting on and Fitting the Bridle

If the bridle is not the horse's own, then a quick assessment of fit is made first before the bridle is put on.

1. The horse should first be tied up in a head collar and lead rope.

2. With the headpiece held in the right hand and the bit in the left, the bridle is held against the side of the horse's face in approximately the position it would be when put on. This is a quick guide. If the bridle is either too long or too short, it can easily be altered by changing the length of the cheek pieces.

3. When the bridle appears to be the right size, prepare it by removing all the straps from the runners and keepers. These are the loops in which the straps are held, the keepers are the static loops, the runners those that move. This makes any alterations much easier once the bridle is on the horse.

4. The reins are placed over the horse's head. The headcollar is undone and refastened around the horse's neck. **At this point the lead rope should be unfastened and left hanging through the string to prevent injury should the horse pull back.**

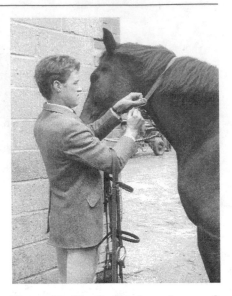

Figure 50: Headcollar is undone and refastened.

Figure 51: Bridle in the left hand, the right arm passes under the horse's head.

5. With the bridle in the left hand, the right arm passes under the horse's head, round to the offside and is positioned about half way down the front of the horse's face.

6. The bridle is now passed to the right hand and held a little below the browband. Some horses have a tendency to raise their heads, evading the bridle and bit, if so press heavily with the right hand on the horse's nose and speak to him firmly.

7. Cradling the bit in the left hand, between the thumb and the second two fingers to hold it apart, place it on the horse's lips. He should open his mouth. If he does not, place the left thumb in the side of the horse's mouth. The horse has a space between the incisor (front teeth) and the molars (back teeth) where the bit normally lies. If the horse still refuses to open his mouth, wiggle the thumb, touch the top palate or depress the tongue.

8. Once his mouth is open, gently slide the bit in, at the same time raising the bridle with the right hand. Holding the bridle steady, gently fold the ears under the headpiece and tease the forelock forward.

9. The throatlash can be fastened and the fit checked by placing a hand widthways between it and the horse's cheek.

10. A cavesson noseband can be fastened and checked for fit. Other nosebands remain unfastened until the bit has been checked.

The Bit

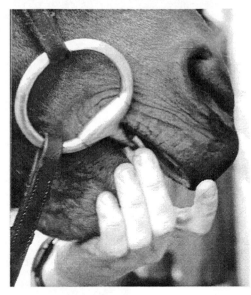

Figure 52: Gently slide the bit in.

Position

When the bit is in the correct position, it should just cause a wrinkle at the corners of the mouth; as though the horse is grinning. If it is too low it will bang on his incisor teeth. Too high and it will be uncomfortable, causing damage to the lips or coming into contact with the molar teeth.

The cheekpieces must be fastened equally on both sides, buckles in the same number holes of the headpiece, so that one side of the bit is not higher than the other.

Size

The width of the bit can be assessed by straightening it within the horse's mouth and placing the tip of each thumb on either side by the horse's lips. There should just be the width of the thumb tip between the lips and the bit rings, approximately a quarter of an inch either side of the mouth. If the bit is too narrow it will pinch the lips or the ring itself will be pulled through the mouth. Too wide and the bit will be uncomfortable, the action within the mouth incorrect.

Once the bit has been checked and fitted, the noseband can be fastened.

Any alterations to the bridle whilst it is on the horse should be done gently and quietly. Once the fit is correct all the straps can be replaced into the runners and keepers.

If the horse is not be used immediately, the bridle is made safe by twisting the reins around each other several times and then by fastening one rein up inside the throatlash. This prevents the horse from getting a leg caught through the loose reins. The headcollar can be replaced and fastened over the bridle and the leadrope fastened with a quick release knot.

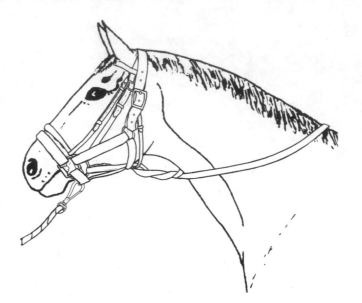

Figure 53: Headcollar over bridle and reins twisted.

Removing the Bridle

Place the headpiece of the headcollar around the horse's neck and fasten the buckle. The leadrope hangs loose through the string on the securing ring.

Unfasten the noseband and throatlash first. Take the reins in the right hand and bring them to the headpiece by the horse's poll. Then, standing in front of the horse, with both hands hold the headpiece and reins either side of the horse's head adjacent to the browband. Gently ease the bridle over the ears.

Slowly lower the bridle. The horse should open his mouth and let the bit slip out. The bridle should never be pulled off roughly or too quickly, as the bit will bang the horse's teeth. Replace the headcollar and tie the leadrope up with a quick release knot.

Note. When tacking a horse up, the bridle should be put on first and then the saddle. When untacking, the saddle is removed first and then the bridle.

Running Martingale

The running martingale is used to prevent the horse from raising or tossing his head beyond the point of control and evading the bit.

Description

This is a 'Y' shaped leather strap with a loop at one end which attaches to the girth. Each of the two thinner straps has a metal ring through which the reins pass. A neck strap, connected via a rubber ring, keeps the martingale in place.

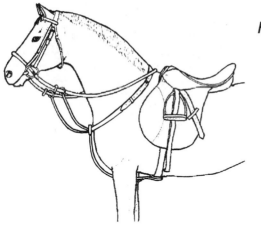

Functions

1. Prevents the horse from raising his head above the level of control.

2. Prevents the horse from tossing his head from side to side.

3. Lessens the involuntary movements from a novice rider's hands.

4. Useful in the training of some young horses.

5. Keeps the reins in place and allows some control in difficult circumstances.

Putting on

Hold the martingale with the buckle of the neck strap on the left hand side, the two straps in front of the rubber ring and the girth loop behind. Now place the neck strap over the horse's head onto the neck. Undo the reins at the buckle and thread each rein through the appropriate ring. Check that there are no twists in the reins and refasten. Each rein must have a rubber stop positioned in front of the martingale ring, to prevent the ring from slipping forward and interfering with the bit. Before fastening the saddle girth, pass the girth loop between the horse's fore legs and pull the girth through the loop.

Fitting

There should be one hand's width between the neck strap and the horse. If the neck strap is too tight it will restrict breathing. Too loose and it will allow the martingale to hang down; it is possible the horse may catch a front leg in the straps.

The girth loop should be central under the horse's belly and flat against the skin; if it is twisted and bent it may rub or pinch.

Check the fitting of the two straps before the reins are passed through the rings. Holding the straps either side of the horse, the rings should just reach the level of the withers. Alternatively, measure the straps by taking them towards the angle of the horse's jaw. With the horse's head in its normal position, the rings should just reach the throat.

If the straps are too short the resulting downwards pull will interfere with the action of the reins. The constant pressure on the bit could also damage the horse's jaw. The two straps may, on occasion, be fitted a little shorter but never more than one hand's width below the withers. The martingale should come into effect only when the horse lifts his head above the angle of control. *It must never restrict the horse's normal action.* If the straps are too long, the martingale will have little effect.

Cleaning the Tack

It is imperative that all tack is clean. Dirty tack causes endless problems for the horse and rider. As well as being uncomfortable and distressing to the horse, dirty tack can cause sores, galls, open wounds, infections, blood poisoning or tetanus. The horse may even end up 'tack shy'. Dirty tack deteriorates, quickly becoming worn and unsafe. All tack should be cleaned after use and have a complete strip down about once a week.

Cleaning is divided into two categories - the 'after exercise' or quick clean and the weekly thorough clean.

After Exercise Clean

The 'after exercise clean' removes dirt, grease, dust, mud and sweat from the surface of the leather. The equipment needed is saddle soap in a bar or tin, a sponge or soft cloth and warm water.

Bridle

It is easier if the bridle is suspended from a cleaning hook. Remove all the straps from the keepers and runners. Wipe the leather thoroughly with a *damp* sponge so that all the dirt is removed. Now wipe the slightly damp sponge over the saddle soap. Avoid creating a lather as this will stain the leather. Rub the sponge over the bridle, pushing the saddle soap into the grain.

The bit is washed in clean water, including particularly the areas around the rings and the joints. Saddle soap should not be used on the bit.

Saddle

The saddle is cleaned after use with the saddle soap and sponge. The numnah is removed and all areas, under the flaps, girth straps and linings given a quick clean. The stirrups can be wiped over and any mud removed.

This type of cleaning should be done every time the bridle and saddle are used but at least once a day.

Girths

A dirty girth causes sores, infections and girth galls. Grit and mud are kicked up from the horse's hooves onto the girth area, so it is particularly important to clean this part of the tack every time it is used.

Girths can be cleaned either by wiping over with a damp cloth or, for leather girths, with a little saddle soap. Most synthetic girths can be washed in the washing machine. All types of girth must be completely dry before use.

Thorough Clean

Once a week the tack should be thoroughly cleaned. This involves stripping it down completely and systematically washing and cleaning all the leather and metal work.

Bridles are taken apart, each piece cleaned separately and the bit washed in clean water. The bridle is reassembled with all the buckles replaced into the correct holes.

Saddles should have their girths, stirrups and stirrup leathers removed, together with the buckle guards. Every part is thoroughly cleaned, including the underneath parts of the skirt, flap, girth straps and linings.

Girths and numnahs should be washed and thoroughly dried.

All metal work, apart from the bit, can be cleaned with a metal fluid.

Once every six to eight weeks the leather will need to be oiled or worked over with a leather dressing. A new bridle may need two or three dressings of oil to make it soft and pliable.

The tack is inspected for any rotten stitching, splitting leather, holes, thin metal work and wear to the bit.

Care of Tack

Bridle

The bridle should always be stored on its bridle holder.

To hang it neatly, pass the throatlash round the front of the bridle, through the reins and around the front again, fastening it to its corresponding strap. This will prevent the reins dragging on the floor and getting dirty. Fasten the noseband around the whole of the bridle to keep everything in place.

Bridles may be carried by placing the headpiece and reins over one shoulder.

Saddle

The saddle should always be handled carefully. When not in use the saddle should be placed on a saddle rack in a cool, well ventilated, dry position. When carrying a saddle, it is easier to carry it on the forearm with the pommel at the elbow. The saddle should never be placed flat on the floor or left lying in damp areas, near extreme heat or in the reach of horses.

Exam Tip

For the examination you should know the parts of the bridle and have a basic understanding of their function. You should be able to recognize and name different snaffle bits. If by some chance in the exam you are questioned about a bit that is unknown to you, do not panic. Instead describe the type of mouthpiece, the thickness of the bit and severity, ring attachments if any and presence or absence of cheeks. You should be familiar with each type of noseband and be able to fit them correctly.

You must be capable of putting on and taking off a bridle and of assessing the fit of the bridle, bit and appropriate noseband. Before the exam inspect both good and ill fitting tack so that you learn the points that need to be noticed. Do this several times until you are confident with all types of tack and its relevant fitting. The examiners may also question you about cleaning, care and storage of bridles and bits.

C H A P T E R   16
Saddlery

Saddles

There are various designs of saddle used for different purposes, such as the showing saddle, child's saddle, side saddle, the long distance, western and racing saddle. These have special features according to their use. However for Stage I, candidates need only refer to the three main types.

The 'General Purpose saddle', as the name implies is used for all types of activities, dressage, show jumping or cross country. The other two are specialist saddles, namely the 'Dressage' and the 'Jumping' Saddle.

General Purpose Saddle.

This is the most popular type of saddle for work where there is a combination of disciplines, such as schooling and hacking, when jumping may be included. It is also very useful for riding schools where a variety of work is performed.

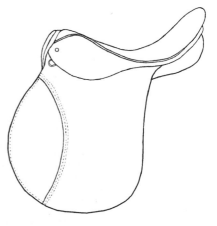

The general purpose saddle has a medium cut flap, that is the flap is cut neither too straight nor too forward, allowing the rider to take up a position for flat work or jumping.

Figure 54: General Purpose Saddle.

Dressage Saddle

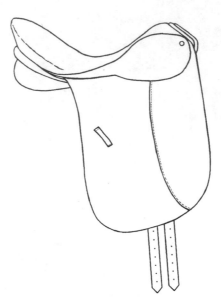

Figure 55: Dressage Saddle.

The Dressage saddle is used solely for flatwork.   It features a straight cut flap encouraging the correct position of the leg and allowing a closer contact with the horse's side.   In some dressage saddles this is further enhanced by having long girth straps which fasten to a short girth.   This girth, called a Lonsdale, fastens on each side of the horse's belly, not under the saddle.   The Dressage saddle usually features a deeper seat.

Figure 56: Leg Position ~ Dressage.

Jumping saddle

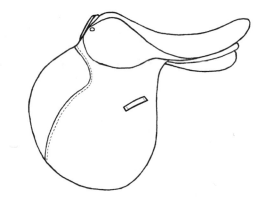

Figure 57: Jumping Saddle.

The flaps for this saddle are more forward-cut, allowing the rider's knee to be bent. There are usually knee and thigh rolls that help to keep the leg in place. The seat is flatter allowing the rider's body to move into the fold position.

Figure 58: Leg Position ~ Jumping.

Structure of Saddle and Material Used

The saddle is based on the 'tree' usually made of **laminated beech plywood** but it can be constructed of other materials such as **plastic or fibreglass**. Bands of **webbing** are stretched along the tree and onto this framework is placed the **stuffing** and the **leather seat**. The stuffing can be made of **wool, felt, foam rubber** or other similar material. The **stirrup bars** are then attached to the tree.

Saddles are usually made of leather, which has many excellent qualities. It is hard wearing, durable, strong and easily cleaned. The new synthetic saddle is gaining in popularity being lightweight, comfortable to ride on, easy to clean and relatively inexpensive to buy.

Points of a Saddle

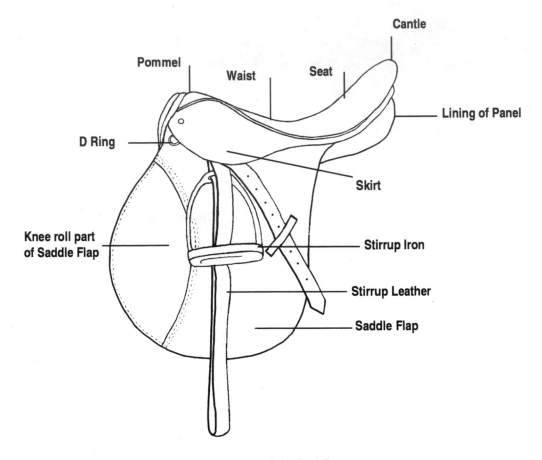

Figure 59: (a) Points of the Saddle.

The **pommel** is the front of the saddle, above the withers.

The **seat** is the part on which the rider sits.

The **waist** is the narrowest part of the seat.

The **cantle** is the rear part of the seat.

The **skirt** is the flap that covers the stirrup bar.

The **stirrup bars** are pieces of metal, one each side of the saddle, from which the stirrups are suspended. These can either be **open ended or have a latch**. This latch, in normal circumstances, remains open allowing the stirrup leather to slip off. This is designed to prevent a fallen rider from being dragged if his foot is caught in a stirrup.

At other times the latch can be turned up, to keep the stirrup and strap in place. This is necessary when the horse is not being ridden - for instance in lungeing or with the led horse in Ride and Lead. *The latch must never be turned up when the horse is being ridden.*

The **saddle flaps** cover the side panels and girth straps. These flaps should be large enough for the rider's legs and the correct shape for the type of saddle.

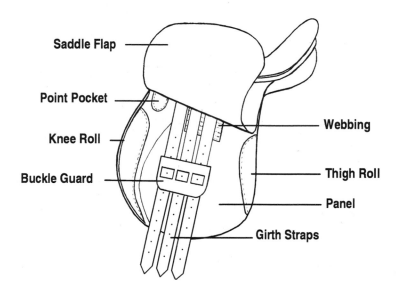

Figure 60: (b) Points of the Saddle.

The **panels** are the bearing surface on the horse's back and sides. The panels in contact with the horse's back are usually stuffed with wool or felt. The panels on the sides are normally thin so that the rider's legs can come into closer contact with the horse. A portion at the front can be stuffed to provide a **knee roll** and at the back, a **thigh roll.** Some side panels are cut short and fully stuffed. This **'half panel'** design is usually used for pony saddles.

There is sometimes a **sweat flap** between the side panel and the **girth straps**.

The **girth straps** are connected to the saddle by webbing strips. Most saddles have three straps, but on some dressage saddles there are only two.

There should be a **buckle guard** which fits onto the girth straps, protecting the saddle flap from marking or damage caused by the girth buckles.

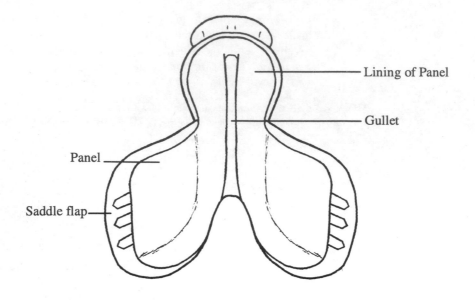

Figure 61: (c) Points of the Saddle.

The **Lining** is the underneath covering of the panels. This is usually made of leather, which is easy to clean and durable if kept correctly. Other materials can be used such as linen or serge, and whilst these are soft and comfortable for the horse they are not as hard wearing or as easy to clean as leather.

Assessing the Condition of a Saddle

The saddle should be regularly checked for condition. This can be done once a week when it is thoroughly cleaned.

The saddle should be inspected for any holes, cracked or split leather. This is particularly important in areas that are potentially vunerable, such as the girth straps and the webbing to which the straps are connected. If the girth straps are worn or split, or have become insecure around the webbing area, the saddle should not be used. Make sure that both sides of the saddle are checked; the nearside and the offside.

The underneath panels should be checked for any lumps or hard areas that may cause the horse discomfort. The side panels are inspected for any holes, split leather or cracks.

The girth is checked for frayed areas, splits, holes or broken buckles. If there is any problem that could make the girth unsafe then it should not be used.

Checking for a broken tree

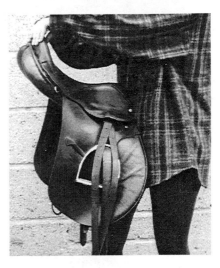

Occasionally saddles are accidentally dropped or trodden on, which may result in a broken tree. The tree is checked by holding the pommel against the stomach and pulling the cantle forwards towards the pommel with both hands. The movement felt in the saddle should be slight. If there is excessive movement or any noise, the tree is broken. The saddle should not be used.

The Pommel

To test the pommel, rest this part of the saddle on the knee and holding both sides flex the pommel inwards and outwards. Any movement, creaking or clicking noises would indicate that the front arch is broken.

Putting on a Saddle

The bridle is put on first and the headcollar over the top. The horse is then restrained with the headcollar and lead rope.

First check that the stirrups are run up the leathers correctly and secured; the stirrups must not slip down and bang the horse.

The girth can be removed and placed on the handler's shoulder for convenience. This is safer for a Lonsdale or short girth that tends to flap around and hit the horse's side when the saddle is placed on top. Most girths can be left fastened to the offside straps and laid over the top of the saddle, as long as they are secure and will not slip.

Pat the horse on the neck and continue to stroke along his back. This smoothes down the hair and prepares the horse for the saddle. There is nothing more off-putting for a horse than to have a heavy saddle dumped on his spine without warning.

Place the saddle gently on the withers and slide it backwards until it lies in the correct position, with the pommel just behind the withers. Again sliding the saddle back encourages the hair to lie in the direction of the coat. Do not allow the saddle to slip too far back into the delicate loin area.

If the girth is completely detached from the saddle, walk around the front of the horse to the offside and fasten the girth onto the straps. Check that the panel and buckle guard are lying flat. Gently place the girth so that it is hanging down by the horse's side.

Return to the nearside, via the *front* of the horse, pat his shoulder and crouch down to reach the girth. Gently fasten the girth onto the straps on the nearside. Watch for any reaction from the horse; some can be quite sensitive. Check that no part of the saddle is bent under or twisted.

The girth should be fastened to the same two straps on each side. These should either be the first and second girth strap or the first and third, *never the second and third*. These straps are attached to the saddle by the same webbing and, should this be damaged or come away from the saddle, then the girth will give way.

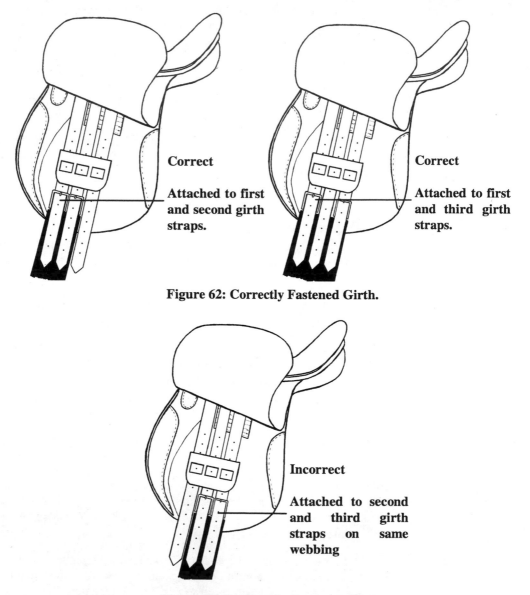

Correct

Attached to first and second girth straps.

Correct

Attached to first and third girth straps.

Figure 62: Correctly Fastened Girth.

Incorrect

Attached to second and third girth straps on same webbing

Figure 63: Incorrectly Fastened Girth.

The girth is tightened gently. This is normally done on the nearside but to prevent the girth being higher on one side than another; it can be tightened on the offside. Ideally the buckles should be on the same number hole on each side and, when the girth is tight, should reach halfway up the straps.

The girth is sufficiently tight when the rider can *just* fit the flat of the hand between the girth and the horse. The girth must always be rechecked five to ten minutes after starting the ride. Some horses are masters at expanding their girth area and it is amazing how much tighter the girth can be fastened.

If the girth is on the very top holes before work commences then the girth is too long and MUST NOT BE USED.

If the girth only just reaches the lowest holes on either side then it is too short. It will be difficult trying to tighten the girth later and if the leather around the hole splits the saddle will no longer be secure.

Checking the Fit of a Saddle

When checking the fit of a saddle, a numnah should NEVER be used.

Size

Check the **size** first. Ask someone to hold the horse; stand back from the nearside and take a general look at the saddle. It should be immediately obvious if the saddle is **too small** or **too big** for the horse.

Too long a saddle will stretch back over the loin area and possibly damage the kidneys.

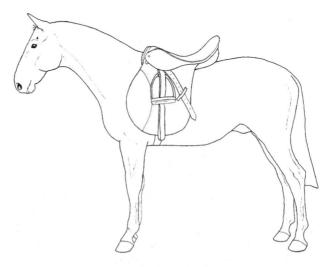

Figure 64: Saddle too Large.

Too large and the saddle flaps and the panels underneath will encroach forward onto the shoulder area restricting the horse's movement. The horse will not have the freedom to move his shoulder properly.

Too short and the rider's weight will not be distributed evenly over the horse's back but concentrated in one area. This may lead to the development of sore pressure points. The saddle flaps will also be *too small for the size of the rider.*

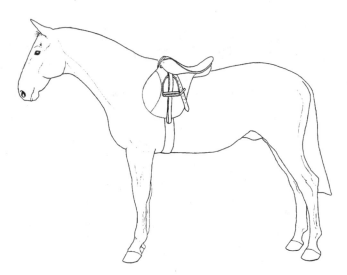

Figure 65: Saddle too Short.

The cantle should be slightly higher than the pommel, (but only slightly or the rider will be tipped forwards into an incorrect position). If it is lower, the saddle is too flat for the horse's shape in which case the gullet will not have enough clearance from the backbone. This will encourage the rider to sit too far back, placing her in an incorrect position and possibly bruising the horse. The saddle may simply just not fit or may need re-stuffing. A professional saddler or tack shop would be able to tell if the saddle needs re-stuffing.

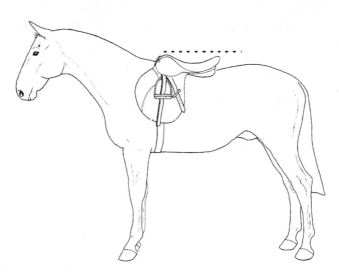

Figure 66: Cantle Too Flat.

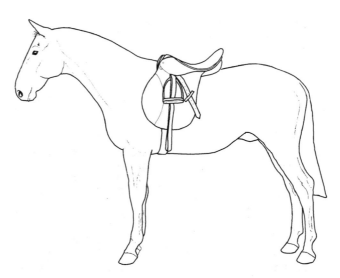

Figure 67: Correctly Fitted Saddle.

The Fit

Now an assessment of the saddle is made in specific areas.

The most important point to check is the space between the saddle and the horse's spine. There are two areas to look at,

1. The front at the withers.

2. From behind the horse along the gullet of the saddle.

The Withers

The pommel of the saddle should be **four fingers width** above the withers with *a rider mounted.* If, therefore, the pommel does not have *at least* four fingers' clearance above the withers, without the rider on top, then it certainly will not fit.

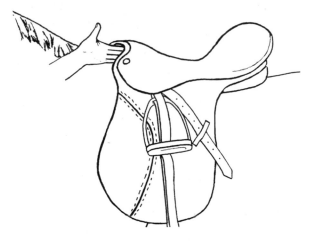

Figure 68: Checking Pommel Clearance.

Check this by inserting the fingers under the pommel between it and the horse's backbone. If there is less than the width of four fingers, the saddle will certainly come into contact with the horse's spine when a rider mounts and flattens it. Pay particular attention to that part of the gullet just behind the pommel. This area sometimes dips and comes into close contact with the horse's spine.

Now check for pinching either side of the withers around the shoulder area. Feel with the tips of the fingers between the panels and the top of the horse's shoulders. The saddle should fit snugly but smoothly. If it is tight and pinching the horse's skin, the saddle is too narrow. If it is too wide, almost certainly the saddle will be too low on the horse's back.

Finally, check for movement of the saddle. Holding the cantle, lift it gently up and down. If the girth is tightened sufficiently there should only be a slight movement. If the saddle can be raised to a large degree it is too wide. This will allow excessive movement when the horse is ridden, making the saddle bang down on the horse's back, particularly with rising trot.

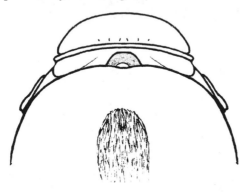

Now move to the back of the horse carefully, to avoid being kicked, and from the hindquarters look along the gullet of the saddle. There should be a clear space all along.

If the saddle comes into contact with the horse's spine at any point it will cause damage and result in pressure points. These are areas of rubbing and bruising causing lumps, soreness and possible ulceration.

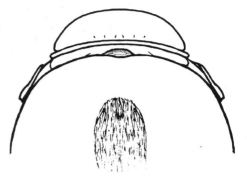

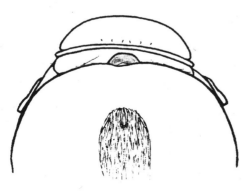

Check also from the hindquarters that the saddle is sitting straight on the back. It should not slant or tilt to one side. More pressure will be applied on this side and the rider will be forced to sit incorrectly.

In Use

If everything is satisfactory, it is correct to ask that someone rides the horse. Once the rider is mounted assess again the space between pommel, gullet and the horse's spine.

The saddle should now be checked from all angles whilst the horse is in movement, to see that it stays quite secure. Particular notice should be taken from the back with the rider in rising trot; the saddle should not swing from side to side or bounce up and down. There must be no excessive movement on the horse's back, as this will cause chafing and bruising.

Incorrectly Fitting Saddles

The perils of an ill fitting saddle are numerous and can be long lasting. Because the saddle is in close proximity to the spine, a very vulnerable part, any discrepancy in the fit could result in problems. These can range from bruising around the spinal area, sores, galls, misalignment of the spine and a 'cold back' that can last a lifetime.

A horse that has a 'cold back' is one who has probably suffered pain from an ill fitting saddle in the past. He may be extremely difficult to tack up, suffer discomfort and become awkward when mounting.

Correct fitting is essential for the mental and physical health of the horse, his freedom of movement, the comfort and correct positioning of the rider. The last point is relevant because any constant incorrect position of the rider can give the horse a sore back and pressure points.

Numnahs and Saddle cloths

In theory a numnah or saddle cloth is unnecessary with a well-fitted saddle but most riders prefer to use one, believing that they are kinder and more comfortable on a horse's back. They also help to keep the saddle clean.

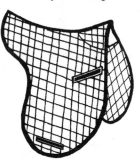

Figure 69: Numnah.

Figure 70: Saddle Cloth.

There are however, a variety of circumstances in which they are useful;

- If the horse's back is 'soft'. This is usually after a period off work when the saddle has not be used for some time.

- If the horse's shape has changed. This again may be after a period off work and is a temporary measure until the horse regains his normal muscular physique.

- If the saddle does not fit correctly, for example when it needs re-stuffing. (This must be corrected as quickly as possible.)

- If using another saddle for a short period. This situation must also be amended as quickly as possible. A numnah should not be used to ease the problems of an ill-fitting saddle.

- If the rider is a learner or novice and does not sit quietly in the saddle.

- In long distance, endurance riding or when the horse is ridden for any length of time.

- With a deep seated saddle that concentrates the rider's weight in a small area.

- With a 'cold-backed horse' to help lessen his fear and to provide a warm, comfortable covering under the saddle.

Putting on the Numnah or Saddle Cloth

The numnah or saddle cloth can either be put on the horse's back separately before the saddle or attached to the saddle first.

If separate, place the numnah on the withers and gently slide it backwards to lay the hair. Place the saddle on top and pull the front of the numnah or cloth well up into the pommel of the saddle. Take the numnah loop under the first girth strap and fasten it around the second strap. This keeps the numnah in place.

Then, picking up both numnah and saddle again, place them forward on the horse's withers and slide back into the correct position. *Make absolutely sure that the numnah stays well up into the gullet of the saddle.* If there is another loop at the bottom of the numnah, pull the girth through or, in the case of a dressage saddle, pull the long girth straps through.

If the numnah is already attached to the saddle, check that the fastenings are correct and secure. Then holding the numnah well up into the gullet, place both the saddle and the numnah onto the horse's withers and slide backwards into position. Once the saddle and numnah are in the correct position, it is now time to check the fit.

A numnah is cut closely following the shape of a saddle. When it is the correct size it will be approximately an inch larger than the size of the saddle all round.

A saddle cloth is usually a square or oblong shape and should be larger than the saddle. It should not be so large as to interfere with the rider when he tries to use his legs or whip.

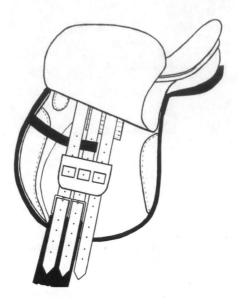

Figure 71: Numnah attached to Saddle.

Untacking the Saddle

Secure the stirrups by pulling the leathers through the irons. Restrain the horse with a headcollar and lead rope.

Unfasten any attachments such as a breastplate. Unbuckle the girth gently on the nearside and allow it to hang down. The girth should not be dropped or it may hit the horse's leg. Any martingale loop should now be slipped off the girth.

Walk around the front of the horse to the right side and fold the girth over the seat of the saddle, otherwise the girth will scrape across the back when the saddle is removed.

Return to the nearside and take hold of the pommel in the left hand, the cantle in the right. Slide the saddle backwards slightly to lay the hair. Then raise the saddle cleanly above and off the horse's back. *It should never be dragged across the spine.* Pat the horse's back to help restore circulation.

The saddle must be placed in a safe spot where it will not be damaged, preferably stored away on a saddle rack. If placed onto the floor for a short while, it is laid gently down pommel first with the girth underneath, and the cantle resting against a wall. If the saddle is incorrectly placed or stored it will become damaged.

Exam Tip

Candidates will be requested to put a saddle on a horse and to comment on the fit. You may be asked to do this individually or in pairs. You should be able to show how to check the fit and to explain your assessment.

When approaching the horse to check the saddle, remember to do this correctly. It is so easy in an exam to become pinpointed on the task in hand and forget the basic rules. The examiners will understand but it will create a good impression if you treat the horse as you would normally.

Whilst checking the fit of the saddle, if at any point you feel that the saddle does not fit the horse, this must be pointed out. Do not be afraid to say what you think but at the same time do not criticize for the sake of it. If it is possible, and there is time, make a quick check of the saddle before it is put on. Look underneath at the condition of the panels and linings.

In the examination, after the check has been made on the horse, you may state that the saddle should now be assessed with a rider on top. This will probably not be possible in the exam but you may be asked to describe what you would look for whilst the horse is being ridden.

In preparation for the exam, look at as many saddles as possible assessing good fit, bad fit and condition. This will increase your confidence and knowledge, which will certainly help in the exam situation.

C H A P T E R   17
Clothing

There are different rugs and blankets for various occasions but the two principal types, the stable rug and the New Zealand, are used in the colder months to keep the clipped horse warm and dry.

During the autumn the horse grows a thick winter coat which, together with the grease and oils that the horse's skin produces, insulates the animal against the extremes of cold, wet and windy conditions. Though many native ponies live out through the autumn and winter months without the protection of rugs, most horses and ponies in work are clipped either completely or partially.

The main reason for clipping is to prevent the horse in work from sweating. This can cause discomfort, distress and ill health. Once the natural coat is clipped the horse or pony needs another form of insulation and protection.

Traditionally Jute Rugs with Under Blankets were used, but the new synthetic rugs are now becoming very popular, being warm, lightweight and easy to clean. The New Zealand rug is worn as a protection for a horse spending time at grass.

Other types of rug include the summer sheet, the woollen day rug and the anti-sweat or cooler rug. New designs and materials are being marketed all the time.

Rug fastenings

There are several different types of straps and fastenings used to keep the rug secure on the horse.

Rollers

A roller is a single strap made from webbing, jute, leather or an elasticated material.

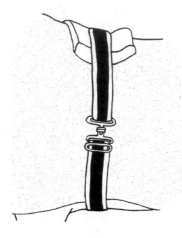

Figure 72: Elasticated Roller.

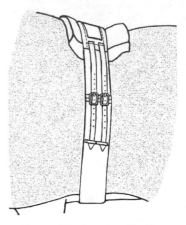

Figure 73: Leather Roller.

Fitting over the back of the horse behind the withers; a roller is fastened either by buckles or a clip on the nearside.

A roller should always have some kind of padding between it and the horse's back to protect the spine. This Wither Pad can consist of one piece of sponge, a thick layer of sheepskin or of two cushioned pads fitting either side of the backbone.

The **Anti-cast roller** has an additional purpose, namely to prevent the horse from rolling over in the box or stable and becoming cast. There is a metal hoop or arch attached to the top part of the roller where it fits on the horse's back. This type of roller can be heavy but for a horse who consistently becomes cast it is a good deterrent.

Fit

To fit a roller, lay it over the horse's back with the longer part to the offside, making sure that the pad is in the correct position. Buckle up on the nearside. The roller should be *almost* as tight as a girth, if fastened too tightly, it can damage the horse's spine.

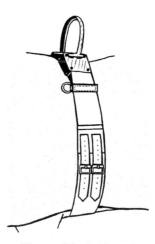

Figure 74: Anti-cast Roller.

Surcingles

Surcingles can either be a single strap or two straps that cross over each other.

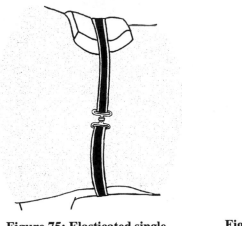

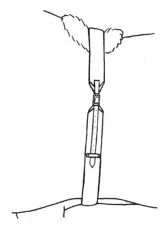

Figure 75: Elasticated single surcingle.

Figure 76: Leather or webbing single surcingle.

Cross-over surcingles are sewn onto the rug, cross under the horse's belly and fasten on the nearside with buckles or clips.

When fastened the surcingles should be tight enough to prevent the rug from slipping off but not so tight as to prevent movement or cause discomfort.

Fillet String

This fits at the back of a rug and is slipped under the tail as extra security.

Normally used on summer sheets or light rugs to prevent the wind from blowing the rug up over the horse's back.

Fillet strings are usually made from plaited cotton.

Figure 77: Fillet String.

Leg Straps

These are fastenings normally attached to a New Zealand rug and worn around the hind legs of the horse. There are two straps, one each side, attached on the inside of the rug at the back. Each strap wraps around a hind leg and is looped through the other strap.

Care in fitting is necessary; too tight and the straps will rub and cause sores. Too loose and the horse may catch a leg in the straps.

When removing a rug a frequent mistake is to forget to undo the leg straps. It is always wise to check, whatever the type of rug. When unfastened, the straps should be clipped to the rings on the same side to keep them safe and tidy.

Figure 78: Leg Straps.

Front fastenings

These can vary quite considerably from buckles, plastic clips, thread-through fasteners or twist clips.

Figure 79: Clip fastener.

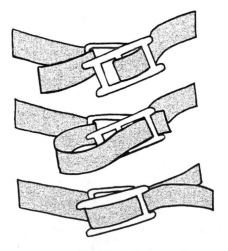

Figure 80: Thread through Fasteners.

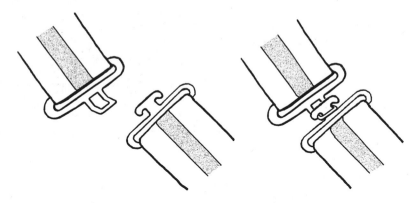

Figure 81: Twist Clip.

Types of Rugs

Jute Rug

This is a traditional rug made of natural jute fibre, either fully or half lined with wool or cotton. Special rot proof Jutes are now available.

The Jute is often worn with a roller, but cross-over surcingles can be sewn on if preferred.

Though traditionally used with an under-blanket, a Jute is quite warm enough on its own.

Jutes are made from natural materials, are hard wearing and warm. They are however, difficult to clean because they shrink.

Under Blanket or Witney Blanket[*]

This blanket is made from wool and is usually a yellow or red colour with stripes.

It is normally used under a Jute rug for extra warmth, though this combination can be quite heavy on the horse.

---

[*] Witney is a registered trade nane.

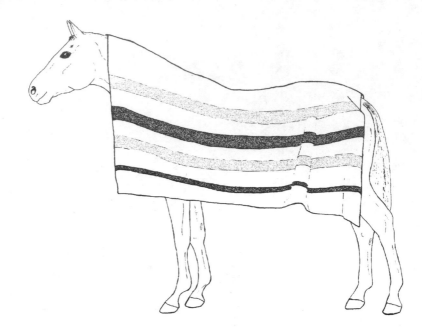

Figure 82: Place blanket high up.

The blanket itself can be a little awkward to fit. To put on; the front of the blanket is placed high up on the horse's neck and folded back, then when the Jute is laid on top, the blanket can be taken back over the front of the Jute.

Figure 83: Fold back.

Figure 84: Secured by a roller.

This type of blanket is becoming less popular. There are now fitted under blankets on the market, many of which are made from synthetic material that is easier to maintain.

Stable Rug

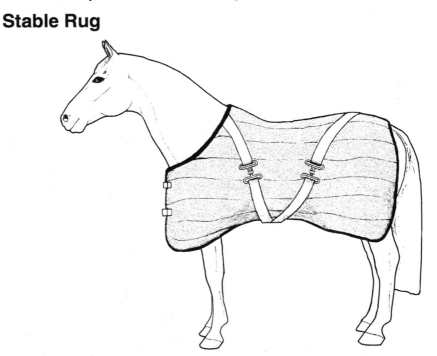

Figure 85: Stable Rug with cross-over surcingles.

An extremely popular rug, the stable rug, night rug or Polywarm* acts like a duvet which is used in the stable during the autumn, winter and spring.

Usually made with an outer covering of nylon, a cotton lining and a fleecy filling, the stable rug is available with varying thicknesses and warmth factors.

The fastenings are normally cross-over surcingle straps around the body, two buckles at the front and sometimes a fillet string.

- A lightweight rug.

- Convenient to use.

- Hard wearing.

- Durable.

- Very easy to clean; it can be washed in a washing machine.

Stable rugs are easily purchased and available in a variety of colours. There are rugs on the market now which claim to take the place of several blankets. These have the appearance of a thick duvet and some include a covering that reaches up the neck of the horse.

Woollen Day Rug

As its name implies, this rug is made out of wool.

During autumn and spring, because it is not as warm as a stable rug or a Jute, the horse can wear this rug on milder days.

The woollen day rug is also used as a smart rug at shows and is often specially made in the owner's colours with a contrasting binding and matching surcingle.

Anti-Sweat Rug

This is a specialised rug used when the horse has become wet either through sweating, in the rain or after a bath. It has the appearance of a large string vest.

Its purpose is to regulate heat loss. The air under the rug is warmed by the horse's body temperature. Whilst a certain amount of this air escapes through the holes, cooling the horse down; some of the air remains trapped under the strands of material, preventing the heat from escaping too rapidly.

It is normally used with another rug on top or with thatching - straw is placed underneath the rug and the circulating air dries the horse.

The Anti-sweat rug can also be used under another rug when travelling.

---

* Polywarm is a registered trade name.

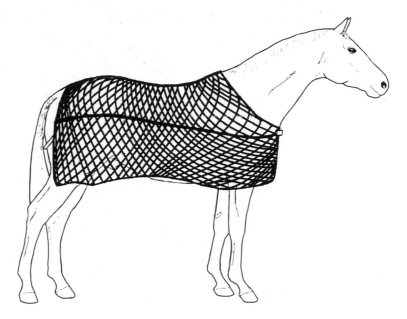

Figure 86: Anti-Sweat Rug.

The Anti-sweat rug, (or Sweat rug as it is more commonly though incorrectly called), is normally fastened at the front with a strap and at the back with a fillet string.

As alternatives there are several new 'cooler' rugs on the market. These have a closer mesh slowing down the rate of heat loss.

Summer Sheet

A thin, cotton sheet worn on cool, summer evenings.

Also used to protect the horse from flies or, when travelling to a show, to keep the horse clean.

The Summer Sheet is fastened by a front buckle and a rear fillet string. Sometimes a light roller strap is used for more security.

New Zealand

This rug is mainly worn by horses out at pasture during the autumn, winter and spring. Occasionally it is worn by horses at grass on wet summer days to keep them dry. A horse should never be tacked up or ridden when wet.

New Zealand rugs come in all shapes and sizes; new designs are introduced onto the market frequently. Some are plain, straight rugs; others have tail flaps to protect the back of the horse from wind and cold. Some include a covering for the horse's neck.

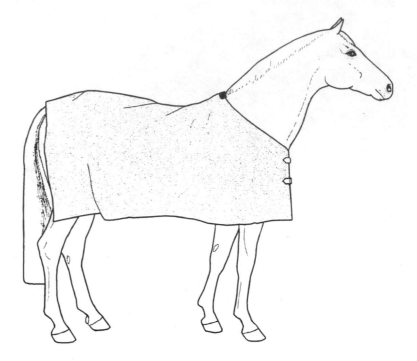

Figure 87: New Zealand.

Made of a waterproof material, usually canvas, and lined with wool, cotton or fleece. The New Zealand needs to be tough, strong and of good quality to survive bad weather and rough usage.

Normally fastened by one or two front buckles, cross over surcingles and leg straps at the rear.

The fit must be correct for the horse to obtain the full benefit of this rug.

Some types are **self-righting** and should remain in place even when the horse rolls.

The New Zealand rug does need special cleaning if the waterproofing is not to be affected. Occasionally the rug will need re-waterproofing which can either be done professionally, or at home with a waterproofing spray.

Often in very windy, wet weather, when the rain gets underneath, the New Zealand can become damp. It is wise to have two New Zealands so that one rug can be dried whilst the other is in use.

Rugs for a Stabled Horse

All the rugs mentioned are the most popular for normal use. A fully stabled horse will need:

1. A Stable Rug for winter, providing it is warm enough to protect against the coldest nights. Alternatives are the Jute rug with or without an Under-blanket.

2. A New Zealand, ideally two.

3. A Summer sheet for the warmer months.

4. An Anti-Sweat Sheet.

Most new horse owners start with the minimum and gradually buy other rugs to add to their stock.

Measuring and Fitting a Rug

Rugs are available in many sizes ranging from those for the smallest pony to the largest horse. It is important to obtain the right size.

A rug that is too small will be uncomfortable for the horse and cause rubbing and sores. A rug that is too large may become tangled in the horse's legs.

Normally rug sizes are available in measurements rising by 3 inches, for example 5 foot 9 inches - 6 foot - 6 foot 3 inches.

To measure a horse for a rug;

a) Use a tape measure or a piece of string.

b) Measure from the middle of the chest right round the side of the horse to a point corresponding to the top of the tail.

c) If this does not fit exactly to a length available in the shop, it is better to obtain a size larger rather than smaller. Experience has shown that rugs do sometimes shrink a little when cleaned and it is no great problem if the rug overhangs the tail slightly.

When the overall length is known, the rug should be checked on the horse for correct fitting.

There should be enough depth of rug to cover the horse's body. Some rugs are the correct length but are too short around the belly. This leaves part of the horse's body exposed and vunerable to the weather.

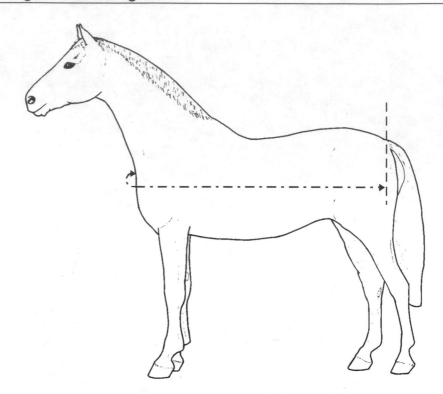

Figure 88: Measuring a horse's length.

It is important that the rug fits around the shoulder, wither and chest area. Check this by placing a hand under the rug at the withers and sliding it right down to the front strap. This area should give the horse plenty of room. There should be no tightness here or there will certainly be rubbing. If the rug is too tight in this area it will be extremely uncomfortable, restrict the horse's movement and result in bare patches and sores around the shoulder. It will be necessary either to get a bigger rug or another design with a different style and cut.

Horses wear rugs for many hours during the winter months and it is essential that a rug fits well.

Putting on a Rug

The rug should be placed on carefully and gently; some horses do object to having a rug thrown on roughly. The safest method especially with an unknown horse or one that is rug-shy is as follows:

> The horse should be restrained by a head collar and lead rope. The surcingle straps of the rug should be tied up so that when rug is put on these do not swing around and hit the horse in his ribs or belly.

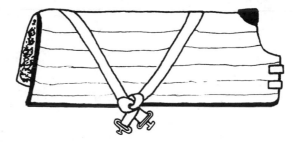

Figure 89: Tie Surcingle Straps.

Hold the front of the rug in the right hand and the rear in the left.

Figure 90: Fold Front to Back.

Fold the front end over the top of the rug so that it meets the back. Straighten the rug and place it over the left arm, front uppermost near the elbow.

Figure 91: Until the front meets the back.

Approach the horse from the nearside shoulder, talking to him quietly. Gently place the quarter of the rug nearest to the horse on to his neck and shoulder, a little higher up the neck than the rug will normally lie. With the right hand take the portion of the rug lying over the left arm and fold it over the withers and the neck so that it hangs down on the offside of the horse.

Figure 92: Place rug on neck and shoulders.

Taking the top half of the rug in the right hand, lay it gently over the back of the horse towards the tail.

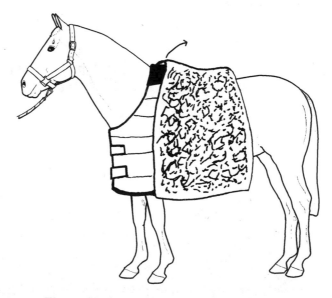

Figure 93: Lay gently over the horse's back.

The front buckles are now fastened.

Slide the rug back; so that the lie of the hair is correct. The rug should never be pulled forward as the hair will bend in the wrong direction. When the rug is in the correct position the front will be just above the withers with the rear reaching the top of tail.

Fasten the surcingles. The straps should be tight enough to prevent the rug from slipping or the horse from getting his legs entangled. But not too tight to restrict movement or cause sores.

If there is a fillet string, gently pull the tail through. Back straps go around the inside of the legs and link through one another to prevent them rubbing and chafing the inside of the thigh.

Check from both sides for folds or crumpled areas.

There is a debate as to which should be fastened first on a rug; the front buckles or the surcingles/roller.

- When the front straps are fastened first the rug can be pulled back on the horse to the correct position before the surcingles are buckled up. If the surcingles are fastened first and the rug is not in the correct position or it shifts slightly, the rug will have to be removed and put on again.

- On the other hand fastening the surcingles first prevents the rug from being blown about on a windy day or from being dislodged should the horse move quickly.

Neither method is wrong but, in practice, the front straps are usually fastened first. The method used depends on practicality and the temperament of the horse.

Removing a Rug

- Unfasten the front straps.

- Undo the straps between the hind legs and clip them onto the corresponding rings.

- Unfasten the centre straps or surcingles.

- Taking the front of the rug, fold it over the horse's back to the tail section.

- Now holding the rug with the front half in the left hand and the back in the right, slide it off the horse's back completely in the direction of the tail.

- The rug can be folded into quarters as mentioned above so that it is ready to put on next time.

Rugs should be hung over a bar or beam or put away in a rug room. Rugs should not be left on the floor or allowed to fall onto the bedding; this is untidy, dirty, and may result in damage to the rug.

Care of the Rug

If a rug is treated and stored properly it will last a long time. All rugs, rollers and accessories should be kept clean and dry, otherwise they can cause skin conditions, infections, rubbing and sores.

Rugs can either be washed in the washing machine and dried outside or taken to the Launderette. Some Tack Shops will clean them professionally.

Great care should be taken with the type of cleaning fluid or washing powder used to clean rugs in case the horse's skin suffers from an adverse reaction.

Rugs should be stored in a dry, cool, well-ventilated area to prevent contamination with mould or fungus.

A horse should never have to wear a dirty, ill fitting, wet or damp rug.

Exam Tip

In the examination there will either be a variety of rugs made available or, during the colder months, a horse wearing a rug. You may be asked to identify certain rugs, to describe them, the materials used and to give the function, advantages and disadvantages. You may then have to put a rug on a horse, show how to measure the fit and remove it afterwards.

CHAPTER 18

Shoeing

A horse's feet are constantly growing. In the natural state this growth is worn away at approximately the same rate by the action of the hoof across the ground. In an artificial environment, with the pressures of work and stress on hard surfaces, the hoof wears away too quickly. It is essential that the feet are protected.

Whilst the shoe protects the horse's foot, it also prevents the natural wearing down of the hoof. The hoof then grows too long causing other problems such as injury, lameness and incorrect action. *All horses regularly need their feet attending to every four to six weeks.*

Here comes another cliché ~ **'no foot, no horse'**. A tremendous amount of weight and stress is placed on the foot. A horse with weak feet is vulnerable to all kinds of problems including intermittent or even permanent lameness.

Foot Structure

To understand shoeing, it is necessary to know the basic structure of the horse's foot.

1.   Horn or Wall

This grows down from the coronet at the top of the hoof, just under the hair. The average monthly growth is about a quarter to three eight's of an inch. It can take 9 to 12 months for a whole new wall to grow. The horn should be healthy and shiny in appearance, with no cracks.

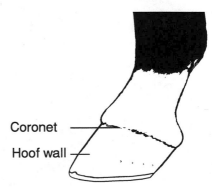

Coronet

Hoof wall

2.   Frog

This is the soft, rubbery portion on the underside of the foot. It is larger at the heel decreasing to a point, roughly triangular in shape. It has an indentation down its centre, *the cleft*, and two hollows either side, *the lateral clefts*. The rubbery texture of the frog helps to absorb concussion; its shape and clefts help to provide grip.

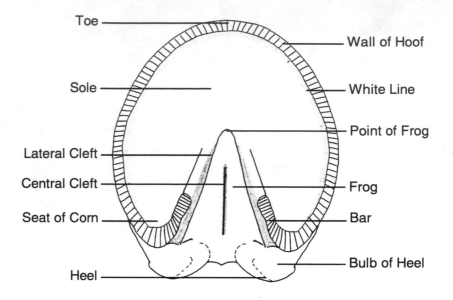

Figure 94: Points of the Foot.

3.   Sole

This is the area of the foot between the frog and the wall. The shape of the sole is important; it should be *slightly concave*. Too flat a sole increases the possibility of bruising, injury and concussion. Too concave a sole and the frog may not come into contact with the ground.

4.   White Line

This is a thin waxy strip on the inside of the wall that separates the sensitive from the insensitive parts of the foot. The farrier uses this as a guide for positioning the nails that secure the shoe.

5.   Bars

These are a continuation of the wall turning inwards at the heel for a short length, parallel with the frog. They help to provide grip.

Shoeing

Shoeing is necessary for a number of reasons;

1. To **protect** the foot from damage.

2. To **reduce concussion** to the foot and leg.

3. To help **correct defects** in **conformation or action**.

4. As part of **veterinary treatment**.

The horse's feet should be cared for by the farrier at least every four to six weeks, even when the horse is unshod and at grass. If left for a longer period, problems will arise with the shoes and the feet.

Indications that shoeing is necessary;

*   The shoe has been **cast;** it has come off completely.

*   The shoe is **loose.**

*   The shoe is **sprung**; barely hanging on by a nail.

*   The shoe has **worn thin** at any part.

*   The **clenches have risen** and stand out from the wall. A clench is formed at the point where the farrier's nail emerges from the hoof. These should be flush with the wall of the foot.

*   The foot is **overlong and out of shape**. A foot is overlong when the wall starts to grow over the shoe. Initially this will begin at the toe.

Many of these defects are apparent just by looking at the foot. When the clenches have risen they will clearly stand out from the wall. It is also quite possible to feel prominent clenches when picking out the foot.

An 'overgrown foot' is apparent when the wall grows over the shoe. In the hind feet the farrier will occasionally shoe this way, setting the shoe back a little. This is to minimize the damage of over-reaching, if the horse has a tendency to do this. Over-reaching occurs when the horse hits his front leg with the toe of the hind.

A sprung shoe may be hanging off the foot. A loose shoe can be heard when the horse moves on hard ground, particularly a road. A worn shoe may be seen when the foot is on the ground but is more usually spotted when the foot is picked up and cleaned. It will appear thin or even cracked in one area. It is easy to check the foot and shoe when daily picking out the feet and this should be done as a routine.

Even if the shoes do not need renewing, the horse will still need its foot trimming. The farrier can remove the shoe, trim the foot and replace the old shoe. This is known as a **'remove'** or a **'refit'**. Some horses need their feet trimming every four weeks, but for most six weeks is sufficient. Horses and ponies at grass may need their feet trimming more often during spring and early summer when the grass is rich and the hoof grows more quickly. If the feet are cared for regularly and the work is carried out by a good farrier, the horse is less likely to suffer problems with its feet or shoes.

The Shoe

Horse shoes, in one form or another, have been used for centuries and today, with new technology, different designs are still being created.

Concave Fullered shoe - (Hunter Shoe)

The most common type of shoe is the 'concave fullered', so called because of its shape and groove.

The inner side of the shoe from the ground surface to the bearing surface, (the part that touches the horse's foot) is slightly *concave*. This imitates the natural shape of the wall and provides extra grip. It also helps to prevent suction from the ground particularly when the conditions are wet.

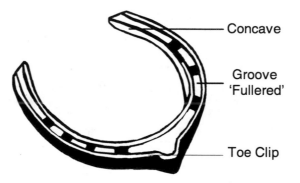

Concave

Groove
'Fullered'

Toe Clip

Figure 95: Front shoe; ground surface uppermost.

The description 'fullered' refers to the groove that is cut from heel to heel on the ground surface of the shoe. This groove not only makes the shoe lighter but also provides grip, particularly on slippery ground.

There are usually seven nail holes, four on the outside and three inside. This number can vary depending on the condition of the foot, the type of shoe, the farrier and the work the horse performs.

There is normally one *toe clip* on each front shoe. The hind shoes have two *quarter clips* leaving the toe free. This is to minimize any injuries caused by over-reaching; to prevent the horse hitting himself with a metal toe clip.

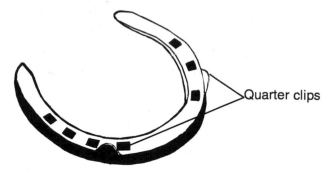

Quarter clips

Figure 96: Hind shoe bearing surface uppermost.

Exam Tip

In the examination you may be requested to inspect a horse's foot and shoe and to describe the condition of both. You may be asked to estimate when the horse was last shod.

Check the shoe first whilst the horse's foot is on the ground. If the foot has recently been shod, the wall will be flush with the shoe and the clenches flat. If the wall projects over the shoe, the clenches stand out or the hoof is cracked and split, the farrier is probably due for a visit.

Pick up the foot and look at the frog, sole and shoe. Feel with your fingers around the hoof for risen clenches, overgrown horn and for wear on the toe or branches of the shoe. This will also indicate approximately when the horse was last shod or if he is due for shoeing.

To prepare for the exam, practise as much as you can by inspecting horses' feet and shoes and, if possible, watching the farrier at work. Most farriers are very helpful and will gladly give valuable information if approached politely and bribed with numerous cups of tea or coffee!

CHAPTER 19

Grassland Management

All horses and ponies should spend time at pasture. Apart from grass being the horse's natural food, time spent in a field will encourage relaxation. Some horses live out permanently while others are given an annual holiday which may extend to weeks or months. Stabled horses in full work usually spend their days off in the field. Whatever length of time the horse spends out, it is important to ensure that all fields provide a safe environment.

What to look for in a field

There are certain aspects of a field that must be assessed before being used for horses:

Fencing

There are two considerations with fencing, the possibility of injury or escape. Fencing that is not properly maintained may pose a hazard and cause injury. Any insecure fencing will allow the horse to escape either by pulling it down, pushing through it or jumping over it.

Post and Rail

This is the most efficient and safest artificial boundary, but probably the most expensive. Wooden posts support two or three wooden rails one above the other. This fencing must be kept well maintained, any rotted posts or broken rails replaced immediately. The wood should also be treated with creosote as a protection against weather conditions and to discourage horses from chewing the fence.

Post and Wire

Less expensive than post and rail. Wooden posts will either support a rail on top and wire underneath or four to five strands of wire. The wire needs to be taut and securely fastened to the posts. The lowest strand of wire should be approximately one and a half feet from the ground to prevent a horse putting a leg through and becoming caught. If the lowest strand is too high the horse may put his head underneath it.

Electric fencing

Generally used to divide fields rather than as a permanent boundary, electric fencing is efficient as long as the horse has knowledge of its position. There is a possible danger to humans, particularly children. One good idea is to cut strips from plastic bin liners and tie these along the wire so that it can be easily seen.

Other Boundaries

Hedges

A natural boundary that must be dense enough to prevent escape, well maintained so it does not become a hazard and free of poisonous shrubs or plants. Hedges can also act as shelter.

Walls

These should be high enough to prevent horses from jumping over and sturdy enough to withstand being knocked down.

Unsuitable Fencing

Some types of fencing should ideally never be used;

Pig or Sheep Netting

This netting is produced by strands of wire that cross vertically and horizontally, creating squares. This can be dangerous as horses tend to put their feet through and become caught.

Sheep posts or stakes

These are made from thin stakes of wood with sharp pointed ends. The sharp points of these posts can cause injuries.

Barbed wire

This type of fencing is used quite extensively around fields where horses are kept and can be a sufficiently good boundary. However sometimes horses do rub themselves on the wire and can sustain quite nasty cuts and scratches. The wire also needs to be checked regularly and kept in good condition. *It must be kept taut.* Horses have ended up with horrific injuries when loose barbed wire has become wrapped around a leg. The horse panics, thrashes about causing the wire to tighten and cut deeply into the flesh.

Checking outside the boundaries is also important as horses can often reach poisonous plants or trees over the fence line. Any defect with fencing or boundaries needs to be dealt with immediately.

The Gate

The gate must be wide enough for animals and machinery to pass through and kept in good condition, so that it can be used efficiently. People should be discouraged from climbing on or over it. This can result in a gate that drops and is difficult to use. All gates should be fastened with a sturdy padlock and a thick chain, preferably at both ends to prevent the gate being taken off its hinges. Horse thefts are on the increase and any weakness around the gate will be exploited.

The position of the access is important. A gate situated on a busy main road is not ideally suitable. It will be dangerous leading horses on the road and it may make horse theft easier. The access needs to be convenient, efficient and safe.

Water

A supply of clean water must be constantly available. This may be naturally by river or stream or artificially by trough or buckets. See the Chapter on Water.

Shelter

Horses at grass must be provided with shelter of some kind, either naturally with trees, a good thick hedge or more ideally with a Field Shelter. This protects them from wind and rain in winter and from heat and flies in summer.

A Field Shelter needs to be large enough to accommodate a number of horses and ponies with ease. It should have a wide entrance to prevent a horse from being boxed in and bullied. There should be a solid approach which will not become poached and slippery. The Shelter needs checking regularly for any defects or damage.

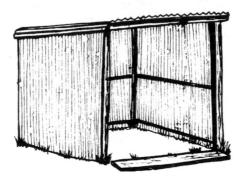

Figure 97: This type of shelter is unsuitable as it does not provide room for a number of horses or ponies.

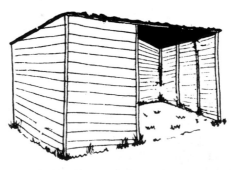

Figure 98: The opening is too small; if a horse or pony becomes trapped inside there could be bullying.

Figure 99: This shelter is large enough to accommodate a number of horses and is open to allow escape from bullying. It also includes a hayrack.

Size of field

The field needs to be large enough to accommodate the number of horses and ponies grazing on it. Too small a field will become overgrazed and horse-sick. When living out and relying mainly on pasture for food, each **horse** needs **one and a half to two acres**, each **pony** needs **one acre.**

Quality of Grazing

A field that has little or no grass on it will not offer the horse any food. He may start eating unsuitable and even poisonous plants, or become thin and ill.

On the other hand grass that is too rich can be just as harmful causing obesity and ill health. Horses do not need lush, rich grass. They need a variety of grasses and a little clover.

Type of Land

The geography of the land is important. Flat land that is liable to flooding is not suitable. The wrong types of grasses will grow in a waterlogged environment and the horse, if stood in wet muddy conditions, may suffer from skin problems such as mud fever or thrush. Undulating land is best, with gentle hills and slopes. This allows free drainage as well as giving the horse some exercise whilst he is grazing.

Hazards

All fields before being used for horses, must be checked closely for possible dangers or hazards. Anything that may constitute a danger must either be removed from the field or fenced off safely to keep the horses and ponies away.

Such hazards include low overhanging branches, rabbit holes, pits, ditches, slippery areas, swamps, bogs, stagnant pools, stakes, sharp implements, rubbish tips with cans or broken glass.

Poisonous plants

There are various plants which, if eaten, are poisonous and can be fatal to the horse. The more common plants are Ragwort, Buttercup, Foxglove, Horsetail, Deadly Nightshade, Hemlock, Purple Milk Vetch, St. John's Wort and Yellow Star Thistle.

Some bushes, shrubs and trees can also be poisonous. These include Privet, Laburnum, Buckthorn, Rhododendron, Yew, Laurel and the acorns from Oak trees.

Any poisonous plants, shrubs or trees should either be removed immediately from the field or fenced off well out of reach of the horses and ponies. If the plants have been pulled out of the ground, they must be removed from the field immediately. Withered, poisonous plants must never be left in the field as they are often more palatable to horses than the live plant.

Grass cuttings should never be fed to horses, eating these can and often does result in colic. Unfortunately many people do dump their grass cuttings in the fields in the mistaken belief that these are good for horses.

Keywords

❖ Fencing

❖ Gates and access

❖ Water supply

❖ Shelter

❖ Size of field

❖ Quality of pasture

❖ Geography of land

❖ Hazards.

Field Maintenance

Daily Inspections

It is important that all pasture is inspected daily, if at all possible, to ensure the safety of the horses and ponies grazing or living in the fields. Fencing should be checked for fallen or rotted posts, damaged railings or broken wire. Natural hedgerow needs frequent inspecting for poisonous plants.

The water supply should be checked daily for cleanliness, the efficient working of the system and the amount of water available. In hot weather horses drink large quantities of water.

The field needs to be inspected for any hazards; fallen trees after a gale, new rabbit holes, boggy or swampy areas after wet weather or rubbish dumped in the field.

Droppings

Ideally all dung should be collected and removed as often as possible. This is to control worm infestation. All horses have worms but with the removal of droppings, together with a regular and correct worming programme, the worm infestation is kept to a minimum. Worm eggs are passed out of the horse in the dung. The eggs hatch and the larvae migrate to the pasture where they are ingested by the horse and the cycle begins again.

In large fields where collection of dung is not practical, the droppings can be harrowed. The harrowing should be done during hot, dry periods in order to kill off the larvae. As larvae thrive in warm, wet conditions, spreading the droppings during these periods will simply increase the worm population.

Worming

All horses and ponies should be wormed regularly at least every six weeks. This is an important aspect of horse care and is closely linked with good Grassland Management. Failure to worm correctly can lead to infestation of the pasture, ill health for the horse and in extreme circumstances even death.

The Horse sick field

Basically a horse-sick field is the result of the owner's negligence. It is bad Grassland Management. Horses are destructive grazers and, if left in a field for too long a period, will quickly spoil the pasture. If the area is overstocked, that is too many horses grazing on it, then the field will quickly deteriorate.

Recognizing a field in such a state is not difficult:

- Bare, overgrazed areas where the horses have stripped the land of nutritious grass.

- Rough spots, usually covered with droppings, where the unpalatable grasses, poisonous plants and weeds grow.

- 'Poached' areas - muddy spots ground up by the horses' hooves, usually around the gate and water trough.

- Trees may often be stripped bare of leaves or bark.

- Fences in bad condition, broken or trampled down by horses trying to feed from the other side of the boundary.

- Water fouled, dirty and green with algae.

- Horses and ponies on the field will look thin, 'ribby', lethargic and ill. They may stand in groups by the gate or fence and be desperately nibbling at the bare ground.

Keywords

- ❖ Overgrazed

- ❖ Excess droppings

- ❖ Weeds

- ❖ Poached

- ❖ Poor fencing

- ❖ Fouled water

Maintaining good pasture

Ideally all fields should be given a period free of horses and allowed to go fallow or be grazed by other stock. Cows and sheep eat different grasses and will crop the rough, unpalatable areas. In addition they digest and kill off some of the worm larva originating from the horses' droppings.

Rotation

This is the method by which the sequence of grazing and 'resting' pasture is alternated over periods of time. For example a large field can be split into three portions, one being grazed by horses, one left fallow or resting and the third being stocked with other animals. These can then be 'rotated' so that each portion has a period of rest, a period being grazed by horses or other livestock. The pasture will then provide good grazing for horses.

Turning the horse out into a field

There is a procedure for turning a horse out which ensures maximum safety. Horses can become quite excitable when being turned out and cause problems for both horse and handler.

The horse should be wearing either a headcollar and leadrope or a bridle. If the field is close to the stables or farm, a headcollar will be adequate for a quiet horse. A bridle is necessary if the field has to be reached by road.

- Walk the horse to the gate quietly. Open the gate wide enough so that the horse does not catch himself. Lead the horse in from the near or offside, whichever is convenient, and shut the gate immediately.

- Take the horse a little way into the field and turn him so that he is facing the gate. Some horses do become excited at this point. *The handler must never be positioned between the horse and the field.* The horse may barge through or inadvertently knock the handler down.

- Standing by the horse's head, quietly slip the restraint off and step backwards. Avoid standing too close to the horse and never slap him on his side or hindquarters, this will encourage him to gallop off and he may buck and kick out.

- Watch the horse for a while until he settles. Fasten the gate properly and check that it is secure.

If two or more horses are being turned out together, they should all be faced towards the gate and released at the same time. If one horse dashes off the others may become excited causing problems for the handlers.

If the horse has not been out for some time, he may want to 'party'! In this case the handler must be prepared and treat the horse with care, avoiding any situation that may lead to injury.

Bringing the horse in

This can again be a difficult time, particularly if the horse is hard to catch or if there are a large number of horses and ponies in the field.

- Prepare the headcollar and leadrope, straightening them out so that there is no fiddling with them whilst trying to catch the horse. If necessary take some pony nuts or a carrot hidden in a pocket. Once in the field the headcollar and leadrope can be hidden behind the back out of view in case the horse feels like playing games!

- Always approach the horse from the front, preferably towards his nearside neck and shoulder. A horse in a field should **NEVER** be approached from behind; he could easily be startled and kick out.

- Holding the noseband, quietly slip the headcollar on and fasten the head piece. If the horse is a little head shy, hold the noseband near his nostrils and allow him to put his nose into the headcollar first.

- If the horse is likely to walk away or mess about whilst his headcollar is being put on, the leadrope can be passed around his neck first. This does seem to quieten down some horses as if they believe the leadrope is a firm restraint. Should the horse jump or move away quickly, release the leadrope immediately.

- If the horse is reluctant to come near, attempt to entice him with the titbits. Alternatively the titbits can be given after the headcollar is on, as a reward. Lead the horse quietly to the gate.

- If possible prevent the other horses from following. When there are a number of horses milling around the gate waiting to push through, it is not only dangerous but frightening. Encourage the other horses to move off, alternatively use another gate or get someone else to help.

Whenever food is taken into a field where there are a number of horses, handlers must be aware of the possible danger. Unless it is absolutely safe or necessary, a bucket of food must not be used to entice a horse. This will definitely cause trouble! The situation can quickly become dangerous, particularly if all the horses gather round and start to fight. It is a terrifying experience being surrounded by a number of horses and ponies who are lunging at each other or kicking.

Some horses can be trained to come to a call. To encourage this, make a noise or call the horse's name whilst he is in the yard and then feed a treat immediately. Eventually the horse will associate the call with a reward and, with any luck, calling him from the gate of the field will be sufficient.

Difficult horses

For the horse who is very reluctant to be caught bringing him in at the same time each day as a part of his routine, can improve the situation.

Alternatively bring him in solely for a treat or feed so that he does not associate coming in with work only.

If the horse is really awkward to catch and tends to run off, great patience is required. Occasionally walking after him (not running or this will become a great game), will eventually convince him that the handler really means business. Take care not to get near his hindquarters in case he kicks.

Some horses are really difficult in which case bringing all the other horses and ponies in from the field may succeed. Horses generally do not like being left alone and, to avoid being separated, the horse may come in with the others.

It may help to turn the horse out in a headcollar. This should only be a temporary measure though as the headcollar can become caught up in fencing or trees. It also makes it easier for the horse thief. As an extra measure a short length of rope (4 to 6 inches) can be attached to the headcollar.

Whatever the circumstances, *safety is of the paramount importance*. A situation where a horse can kick or cause injury must be prevented at all costs. Catching a really difficult horse requires patience and determination but the horse must never win. He should be caught eventually or he will learn to evade and become undisciplined.

Safety in the field and paddock

Regular checks and maintenance within the pasture and boundaries saves a lot of problems later. Handling horses correctly when feeding, taking in or bringing up from the field correctly and knowing how to deal with awkward animals helps to prevent accidents and injuries.

Feed times

During the colder months horses and ponies living out permanently need to be given extra food. The herd tends to crowd around the gate or wherever the food is put into the field. There may be barging, kicking, squealing and fighting. To minimize the risks to horses and handlers there are safety measures that can be followed.

- Always put out as many feed buckets as there are horses, one extra if possible. This helps to prevent bullying.

- Space feed buckets out so that the horses have adequate distance between each other.

- Place hay piles a good distance from each other.

- Place a couple of extra piles of hay than the number horses.

- If feeding one or two horses in a herd, it is safer to take them out of the field and feed them somewhere else.

- Never take a bucket of food into the middle of the herd.

With good grassland management, handling and care the field should provide a safe, healthy and peaceful environment where horses can relax and graze.

Exam Tip

Observation is important for assessing Grassland Management. Visit various fields and make notes of the relevant points - fencing, gates, poached areas, water systems. List the good and bad points; learn to be critical. Look for the poisonous plants and shrubs; most of these are quite common and will be easily identifiable.

Turning out and bringing horses in from the field is a daily event for some owners and riders but if you do not have the opportunity, then practise doing this correctly.

C H A P T E R   20
Safety and Accident Procedures

Accidents do happen in any sphere of life and working around horses is potentially a dangerous occupation. The BHS emphasises safety in every aspect of Horse Management. In Stage I a specific amount of time is devoted to this subject when candidates are questioned about safety in the yard, when on a hack or riding on the public highway. Candidates will also be expected to know about fire precautions and accident procedures.

The first part of this chapter will deal with safety precautions in the yard, in the stable and around horses. The second part deals with accident procedures and the actions to take in the event of an accident.

Safety Precautions

The yard can be a dangerous place. For humans because horses are large, strong animals that can cause injury if not handled properly; for horses because they can react suddenly to situations and may injure themselves or others. All persons working with and around horses, all those learning to ride and indeed everyone, whether partaking in some capacity or merely watching, must be made aware of the possible dangers.

Many establishments have a list of safety precautions in the yard. Making people aware and teaching them the correct method of handling horses minimizes the risk of accidents.

Safety in the Yard

Clothing   Suitable clothing and footwear should be worn at all times and jewellery kept to a minimum.

All tack and horses' clothing should be checked regularly and properly maintained.

Equipment   All personnel must be instructed on how to lift weights correctly and to use equipment and machinery safely.

All stable equipment must be kept clean and in good working order.

Equipment and machinery must be cleared away after use. It should never be left lying around the yard or in the horse's box.

Handling	All horses should be approached and handled correctly at all times.
	Personnel must be taught never to walk around the back of a horse or at least to allow plenty of room.
	Handlers should never kneel or sit on the ground when working around horses, nor place their hands on the floor near the horse.
	Horses should always be enclosed or restrained correctly.
Fire	There must be **NO SMOKING** on or near the yard.
	Fire fighting equipment must be easily accessible and in working order.
	All staff must be instructed regularly on the use of fire fighting equipment.
	All electrical wires must be kept out of the horses' reach and correctly insulated.
	Rubbish and litter must never be left on the yard but removed immediately.
The Yard	All buildings, loose boxes, tack rooms, feed stores and all surrounding areas must be kept clean and free of obstructions
	Noise and activity must be kept to a minimum on the yard.
Emergencies	All personnel must be given instruction on dealing with emergencies.
	The telephone numbers for the Vet, doctors and hospitals should be easily accessible.

Safety in the Box or Stable

All new staff must be shown how to work around horses safely. This subject was covered under the section concerned with handling horses but here are a few of the more important points to remember.

❖   Always tie the horse up when working around him or with him.

❖ Work in the box, muck out, skip out and set fair beds whilst the horse is out if possible.

❖ Always tether the horse to a piece of string which is tied to a solid object (e.g. a ring), never tether a horse directly to a solid object.

❖ Always be attentive and aware when working with horses, avoid dangerous situations.

Safety when Hacking

It is always safer to hack with someone else, but this is not always possible.

If hacking out alone:

❖ Always let someone at the stables know your approximate route.

❖ Take some form of identification, preferably in the pocket of a jacket. It is usual to have your name and address inside your hat, but in the case of an accident the hat should never be removed unless it is absolutely necessary.

❖ The horse should also have some form of identification on him; the name and address of the stables in case he is found on his own. This could be a card inside a plastic luggage label fastened to the saddle or bridle.

❖ Take some form of first aid kit if possible. Carry a **clean handkerchief**; a piece of **string or twine**, a **lead rope** and a **folding hoof pick**. A spare stirrup leather is also an excellent idea.

❖ Take some **money,** or a **phone card** for the telephone. If you are fortunate to own one, a **portable phone** properly secured in a pocket is very useful when out alone.

If in charge of a hack:

❖ Check all the tack on the horses and ponies in the ride. If someone else has tacked up, never assume that this is correct. Make sure everyone's girth is tight enough and stirrups are the correct length. The girth and stirrups should be checked again about five minutes after the start of the ride.

❖ Inform the person in charge at the stable, or another responsible person, the route the hack will be taking, and the approximate return time.

❖ Take two lead ropes, a clean handkerchief, hoof pick and some money for the telephone, or a portable phone if possible.

❖ Always carry a whip.

❖ Never try to do anything that may be risky or potentially dangerous. *The standard of the hack should be that of the least experienced rider on it.*

Safety for Children

Children have little perception of danger. Also many of them tend to look upon a horse or pony as a pet and are astonished when this 'pet' acts, whether aggressively or not, in a manner that causes the child harm. Children often take little notice of adult warnings and have to learn from their own experiences. It cannot be stressed too strongly that any horse or pony has the capacity to hurt and injure a child severely. Warnings must be given constantly and firmly.

As well as the basic rules for working around and handling horses, children should be taught;

❖ **Never** to walk around the back of a horse or pony. This may seem elementary to an adult but frequently children do not know this basic golden rule.

❖ To wear correct clothing at all times and preferably a body protector when riding.

❖ To be quiet and calm around horses. Never to run, shout or act in a loud and aggressive manner.

❖ To avoid feeding titbits. If it is necessary to give a treat, the child should be taught to do so with the hand flattened out to prevent the horse from biting a finger.

❖ Never to get in-between two or more horses.

Fire Precautions and Regulations

Stables are particularly vulnerable to fire because the materials used are very flammable. For the same reason if a fire starts, it usually spreads very quickly and needs prompt, competent action to control it. *It is vital that in any establishment there are regular, frequent fire drills for staff and customers.*

1. Instructions for the fire drill should be clearly visible.

2. Fire fighting equipment, extinguishers, fire hoses, fire buckets filled with sand or water, should be placed around the yard in easily accessible positions.

3. All staff should know where the extinguishers are and how to use them.

4. The whole yard should be kept scrupulously clean and free of litter and rubbish.

5. All entrances and exits should be marked, clear and free of obstructions.

6. There should be **NO SMOKING** anywhere near the stables or yard, around hay or straw.

7. '**NO SMOKING**' signs should be displayed clearly around the yard and strictly enforced.

8. All electric cables, wires, insulation, switches and lights should be frequently checked and well maintained.

9. All doors, particularly of stables, should be in proper working order and if necessary oiled so that they work efficiently.

10. Any bonfires should be kept well away from the stables, under control and supervised until extinguished. A spark carried by a high wind can set alight a bale of hay or straw.

11. Hay and straw should never be kept in the stable block or near stables or loose boxes.

12. All staff should be taught to telephone the Fire Brigade quickly and efficiently giving all the correct relevant information. A display card by the phone giving all the necessary information is extremely useful.

Fire can cause panic; but with frequent practice of the fire drill, correct action will be automatic.

The Public Highway

Safety on the road is absolutely necessary. So many horrific accidents could be prevented if safety rules and regulations were strictly followed.

Leading a horse on the road

❖ If the horse is wearing **tack**, this must be in a **good condition** and **fitted correctly**.

❖ If the horse is untacked then he **must** be led in a **bridle.**

❖ The horse's shoes must be in good condition and secure.

❖ All handlers must wear a **hard riding hat, boots and gloves**.

❖ Horses must be led on the offside so that the handler is between the horse and the traffic.

❖ Considerate **drivers** must always be **thanked.**

Riding on the Road

❖ Never ride on the public highway if the horse is likely to misbehave. All roads, and certainly main or busy roads, must be avoided if the horse is nervous or traffic-shy. If the horse is temperamental ride on the road in the company of another; on the inside of a quieter, more experienced horse and rider.

❖ All tack should be well maintained and fitted correctly. The horse's shoes must be in good condition.

❖ The riders should wear the correct clothing, riding hat, boots and gloves. If the weather is cold and a jacket is worn, this must be fastened properly. It is also wise to wear a body protector. A whip should be carried in the right hand; on the offside.

❖ The pace must be kept steady. Roads can be slippery especially in certain weather conditions. Keep the pace to a walk around corners and roundabouts.

❖ Be attentive and aware of surroundings. Keep a sharp lookout not only on the road but also in surrounding areas, hedges, gardens and behind fences.

❖ Thank all considerate drivers. There are plenty of inconsiderate drivers on the road; those that wait, slow down and give a wide berth deserve thanking.

❖ Groups should keep together and avoid becoming strung out or separated. It is possible to split large groups into two rides. With any number there should be a competent rider and horse at the front and the back of the ride. Novices should be kept in the middle.

❖ Riders and horses need to be clearly seen. This is particularly important in murky weather or at dawn, dusk and essentially at night.

❖ The ride should never be more than two abreast and on narrow roads should be kept to single file.

❖ All riders on the public highway should know the highway code and obey traffic signals and the police.

The Country Code

All land these days belongs to someone, farmers, landowners, County Councils, Forestry Commissions and other authorities. To prevent horses from being prohibited from country areas all riders must avoid damaging property, destroying vegetation and areas of natural beauty, causing injury or loss to livestock and from hurting or frightening pedestrians. Through consideration and courtesy from all riders, authorities may be encouraged to introduce and maintain bridleways, offering riders a greater freedom within the countryside.

Where there are designated bridleways riders should stay on these and not stray into footpaths or restricted areas. Horses churn up the ground, particularly in wet conditions, destroying plant life and causing problems for pedestrians.

Rules of the Country code:

❖ Riders should leave all gates as they found them; if a gate was shut then the rider must shut it after passing through.

❖ Riders must keep to bridle ways through fields or ride around the edge. Horses must never be ridden over crops.

❖ Livestock must not be disturbed.

❖ Fence, hedges, walls and gates must never be damaged.

❖ Litter must never be dropped and left lying around.

❖ All risks of fire must be avoided.

❖ Dogs must be kept under control. It is not a good idea to exercise a dog whilst riding as the dog cannot be kept under strict control from horse back.

Most safety precautions are just common sense but it is easy to become complacent in familiar surroundings with a horse who is usually well behaved and docile. Accidents do occur causing injuries which at best are mild and at worst can be fatal to both horse and handler. Safety procedures and precautions should be a matter of habit; they should be strictly enforced from the start with children and new staff, then safety will become a way of life not a chore.

Accident Procedures

When an accident does occur there are proper procedures to follow which will minimize the effect of the accidents, prevent further injuries and keep panic down to a minimum.

In any kind of accident there are four priorities to follow:

1. **Assess the situation.**

2. **Prevent any further accidents.**

3. **Assess the casualty.**

4. **Send for Help.**

Situation   In the first few seconds after an incident it is vital to try and ascertain exactly what has happened. Look around for a few seconds take in all the information available.

Accidents   Assess the surrounding area to discover if there are other problems that may arise. The other riders and horses may be nervous. The ride may need to dismount or you may need to ask someone capable to go for the loose horse. There may be pedestrians close by who can offer aid. If riding on the road you may need to stop the traffic and ask for help. The first few seconds are vital if you are to prevent a catastrophe, it will also give you time to calm yourself and others around you.

Casualty   When the whole situation has been taken under control you must now assess the casualty. Fortunately in most cases the casualty is not badly injured. The fallen rider may have got up by now, no worse than bruised or shaken. Assess the injured party by asking how they feel and then make the decision as to what to do next.

Help   You must never try and deal with a situation that is beyond your capabilities. It is not your job to give medical treatment or advice. If there is the slightest doubt, even if the injured person seems perfectly healthy, it is wise to have them medically examined sometime in the future, or at least advice them to do so. In cases where medical help is needed immediately, send for help and wait until a professional medical practitioner arrives.

In any incident keeping the four priorities in mind, follow the BHS Accident procedures.

If there is an accident whilst hacking

1.   Keep calm. Evaluate the situation and use your common sense.

2.   Dismount and hand your horse to someone capable.

3.   Dismount the rest of the ride if necessary and safe.

4.   Go quietly and calmly to the casualty.

5.   Get someone competent to catch the loose horse.

6.   If necessary send for help.

Whilst on the Highway

1.   If it is necessary to stop the traffic, send one capable rider up the road and another down the road to halt vehicles.

2.   Keep the rest of the ride calm and safe.

3.   Assess the injured rider and if necessary dismount and go to the casualty. If the rider is uninjured and able to remount, take the ride home quietly.

4.   If the casualty is injured, call for help immediately. The police may have to be informed.

5.   If there is a loose horse on the road inform the police.

6.   If the horse is injured, call the Vet.

Injuries

Occasionally injuries are inflicted which need medical treatment. *Under no circumstances, unless you are a qualified First Aider or a medical practitioner, should you give medical treatment of any kind.*

Remember the priorities

Assess the situation   there may be a qualified First Aider around, a pedestrian, motorist or one of the ride. If so let them look after the casualty.

Prevent further Accidents   Keep the people around you safe and calm.

The Casualty

If there is no-one qualified around then you may have to look after the casualty, until some one more qualified arrives. In certain circumstances it may be imperative that you give simple First Aid though it must be stressed that this must only be in life threatening situations. However, an elementary knowledge of the basic steps for profuse bleeding or unconsciousness can not only save a life but can give you confidence when dealing with such a situation.

If the rider is injured but conscious:

❖   Keep the casualty calm and comfortable.

❖   Talk to the casualty, ask if there is pain and where. Obtain as much information as possible as to how the casualty is feeling. Be observant look for obvious signs such as broken bones or bleeding.

❖   It may be necessary to stem any serious bleeding.

❖   Keep the casualty warm by using a jacket or coat as cover. The casualty may be in pain and suffering from shock.

❖   **GET HELP!**

To Stem Bleeding

Apply direct pressure to the wound using a clean handkerchief or other material. Elevate the wounded limb if at all possible.

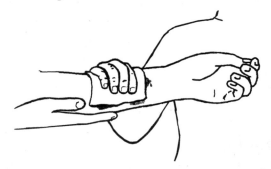

NOTE: DO NOT use a tourniquet. If applied and maintained incorrectly the tourniquet can make the injury worse, it can make the bleeding heavier or damage bodily tissues, possibly even cause gangrene.

Injured Horse

If a horse is injured, assess the injury if possible. Stemming serious bleeding is basically the same as human first aid. Lead the horse home or to safety if he is able to walk without worsening the injury. Seek more experienced advice as soon as possible.

If the Casualty is Unconscious

1. **SEND FOR HELP IMMEDIATELY**.

2. Go to the casualty and check the RESPONSE. Call the casualty's name and gently shake the shoulders. There are many states of unconsciousness; it may be possible that the casualty revives. If this is the case, keep the casualty still, warm and calm until help arrives.

3. If the injured person remains unconscious, OPEN THE AIRWAY. An unconscious person is at risk especially if lying face-up, because they cannot cough or regurgitate to clear the airway. They lose control over the muscles that keep the airway open; the tongue can slip back and block the throat.

4. Check the casualty's breathing by watching the rib cage and feeling for breath by placing your cheek near the casualty's mouth.

5. Stem any serious bleeding.

6. Put casualty into the recovery position.

To Open the Airway

1. Clear the airway of any obstruction. Look into the casualty's mouth to see if there is a blockage and remove anything obvious.

2. To open the airway; put two fingers under the chin and one hand on the casualty's forehead and tilt the head back gently.

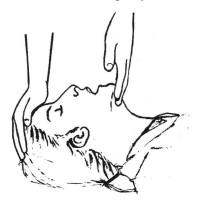

Recovery Position

1. Make absolutely sure that the airway is open. Straighten out the casualty's legs.

2.   Kneel beside the casualty and take hold of the nearest arm. Bring it out at right angles to the body and bend the elbow.

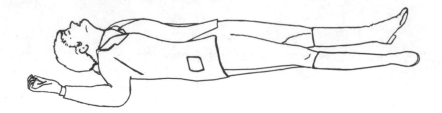

3.   Take the other arm and bring it across the chest. Lay the hand, palm outwards, against the cheek nearest to you.

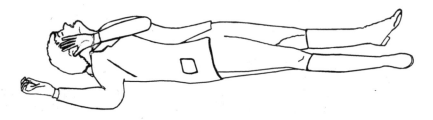

4.   Gently take hold of the farthest leg just above the knee and bend it.

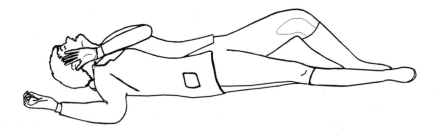

5.   Now holding onto the leg and keeping the casualty's hand against the face, gently roll the casualty over towards you. Keep the bent leg at right angles to the body so that the casualty cannot roll too far.

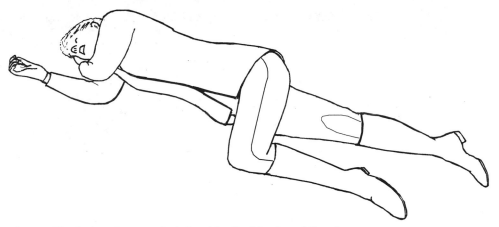

6.   Check that the casualty's head is tilted back and the airway open.

7.   Cover the casualty with a coat or jacket.

The recovery position is vital if, for any reason, the casualty must be left alone whilst you get help. Any unconscious person should not ideally be left but there may be circumstances when this is unavoidable.

Fire

If there is a fire in the stable or yard DO NOT attempt to put it out unless you are sure you can do so correctly and completely. Never put yourself at risk. A small fire may be put out with an extinguisher but, **if there is any doubt**, get everyone to safety first and call the Fire Brigade.

A fire in a yard with horses is a horrendous experience. Get help immediately. Open all the doors of the stables to let the horses out. It may be necessary to close the yard gates to prevent the horses from rushing onto the road. If possible get them into a field or a safe place where there is air and they will not suffer from smoke or fumes.

If it is absolutely necessary to go into the stable to get a horse out; take a headcollar and a jacket to place over the horse's head in order to lead him quietly out of the stable. If, however, this action puts human lives at risk **then it must not be attempted.**

A fire in a yard can spread more quickly than may seem possible. The emergency services must be brought in as a priority.

Sending for Help

Whenever professional help is needed the person telephoning should state:

❖   The telephone number.

❖   Exact location of the accident.

❖   The type and seriousness of the accident.

❖   The number of casualties involved.

❖   As much information as possible about the injured, their possible ages, sex and any medical knowledge that is available.

❖   Details of any dangers or obstacles within the area.

If you have sent someone to telephone for help, ask them to return and confirm that help is on its way.

Accident Report Book

Any incident, no matter how trivial, must be recorded within the Accident Report Book. All establishments must have an Accident Report Book and BHS Accident Report Forms for accidents occurring on the public highway.

The incident must be recorded as follows:

• Date and time that the incident occurred.

• Name of the casualty if any or of any person involved.

• Name of the horse involved.

• Name of any witnesses, their address and signature if possible.

• Details of the accident, giving the facts only, not impressions or accusations of blame.

• Injures if any sustained.

• Action that was taken at the time and by whom.

• Results - whether the casualty was taken to hospital or was given treatment and if the casualty accepted treatment.

• Name of the person in charge of the lesson or hack and their signature.

Later on more information can be added such as a stay in hospital and the length of time it took the casualty to recover.

If it is necessary to complete a BHS Accident Report form, this should be sent to the BHS Road Safety Officer when completed.

Exam Tip

This may seem to be a large amount of information for Stage I, but the BHS are rightly concerned about safety and procedures in cases of accidents. Candidates will be asked about safety rules and accident procedures and may be given an hypothetical situation such as; if you were riding out with a friend who falls off their horse, hits the head and is lying unconscious what would you do? Would you remain with the injured party or leave?

Although it is not necessary to take a First Aid course for the Stage I, learning about the basic first aid procedures benefits everyone, in whatever walk of life. For information on courses contact your local British Red Cross, St. John's Ambulance or St. Andrew's Ambulance Association.

CHAPTER 21
Exam Information

For many, the BHS Stage I is the first experience of this type of examination. Almost everyone takes exams at some time, but the BHS Stages are different. The various sections, riding, practical/oral and theory, are performed in small groups of four or five candidates in front of examiners. For some it is a daunting experience but with study, practice and correct examination technique it can be less arduous. With good preparation, these examinations can often be an enjoyable event!

Prior to the Examination

Prospective students can obtain directly from the British Horse Society some useful publications to help them in their training and study. The 'Where to Train Directory' lists approved training establishments and the Examination Starter Pack includes the syllabus, application form and the current fees. A list of Exam centres and dates for Exams may also be useful. Students, if they are not already a member, will need to apply for British Horse Society membership; an application form can be obtained from the BHS.

The address is:

> British Horse Society,
> British Equestrian Centre,
> Training and Education Dept.,
> Stoneleigh Deer Park,
> Kenilworth,
> Warwickshire CV8 2XZ
>
> Telephone 01926 707700

Applying for the Stage I

Before the application is made, the student should be assessed by a BHS qualified instructor who will check if the standard, especially in riding, has been attained. This will allow time for training and improvement before the examination. Ideally on the day the student should be above the grade required as 'exam nerves' can have quite an effect on ability!

The application for the Stage I must be completed in plenty of time as test centres book up quickly.   The date and venue of the examination should be decided and the application forwarded at least three months in advance. Candidates can telephone the BHS before sending the application form to check if the chosen centre has places available. Other centres and dates can be given as alternatives on the application form.

The BHS will forward a confirmation letter once the application has been accepted. The notes accompanying this confirmation should be read carefully.

Preparation for the Exam

The essential point is to choose a good training establishment with BHS qualified instructors. If at all possible, the candidate should have a few lessons at the chosen Exam Centre where the instructors will know the exam format and the points that the examiners will be assessing. At least then on the 'big day', the centre will not be totally new and unknown!

Clothing

Candidates need to make sure that they have the correct clothing and equipment. All clothes worn on the day need to be smart and clean. For riding this should be a hacking jacket, shirt with a collar, tie, beige jodhpurs, long boots or jodhpur boots. For Stage I a sweatshirt or a v-necked jumper on top of a collar and tie is permitted as are different coloured jodhpurs, providing they are not too gaudy! A secure BSI approved hat and a pair of gloves are compulsory. Whips must be no more than 30 inches in length. Hair should be neatly tied back or contained within a hair net.

Riding Hats

The new standard riding hat, the PAS (Product Approval Specification) 015, (EN 1384) is now compulsory at all BHS Examinations.   There are a variety of designs incorporating this standard of hat, skull caps worn with a silk, or designs similar to the traditional type of riding hat. The hat should also fit correctly.

During the Care Section a waterproof jacket may be worn but this must be properly fastened. Long hair must be tied back away from the face.

The only jewellery allowed to be worn is a wedding ring. Earrings or studs in pierced ears are not permitted.

The Day of the Examination

All candidates need to arrive at the Test Centre in plenty of time. Ideally this should be at least 30 minutes before the start of the exam. Being late creates stress and gives the examiners a bad impression.

If the Centre is unfamiliar, it is helpful to plan the route beforehand, if possible by visiting the venue before the exam day. Candidates do occasionally turn up late after losing their way, a mishap that does not offer an auspicious start! Candidates who are particularly late, may even be barred from taking the exam.

Some candidates have found it helpful to book a lunge lesson, an hour or so before the commencement of the exam. This can help to supple and loosen tight muscles and calm the nerves. Enquire at the chosen Centre about this soon after the BHS have confirmed the date and venue.

Format

When everyone is present each candidate is given a number and a name badge for identification. Candidates may be nervous, but be assured the examiners will be encouraging and give every assistance possible.

The Stage I examination normally begins at 08.30 a.m., and continues until 12.30 - 1.00 p.m. Groups are formed of four or five persons who take the appropriate sections together. The results are given about 15 minutes after the end of the examination.

A timetable on display at the centre will show the order and timings for each section.

BRITISH HORSE SOCIETY STAGE I EXAMINATION		
Timetable		
09.00	Candidates 1- 6	Ride
	Candidates 13 -18	Practical
	Candidates 7-12	Practical/Oral/Theory
10.00	Candidates 7-12	Ride
	Candidates 1- 6	Practical
	Candidates 13-18	Practical/Oral/Theory
11.00	Candidates 13-18	Ride
	Candidates 7-12	Practical
	Candidates 1 - 6	Practical/Oral/Theory
12.00	Finish. Examiners confer	
12.30	Results	

Figure 100: Example of an Examination Timetable.

When everyone is ready, each examiner will take a group to a specific part of the centre where each session begins.

The British Horse Society

The British Horse Society, a registered animal welfare charity formed in 1947, is internationally recognized as the premier Equestrian organization in the United Kingdom. The BHS incorporates the Pony Club.

The BHS is involved in animal welfare, safety, training, rights of way and all aspects of horse care.

Aims

The BHS aims to improve the quality of life for all horses and ponies, preventing cruelty and neglect by;

- Systematic training and education in all aspects of riding and horse management.

- Offering guidance and help throughout with breeding and training of horses and ponies.

- Encouraging the protection of all horses and ponies.

Training and Education

The BHS training and education system is one of the best in the world. It offers training to a very high standard of proficiency and provides recognized qualifications for the industry. It also ensures that approved riding schools and establishments maintain a good standard.

Benefits for Members

Members have a governing body which helps and advises them and through which they can communicate to the higher authorities, for example the Government and the EEC.

Members are entitled to a free Personal Liability and Accident Insurance and access to a legal and tax helpline which gives advice. They are also entitled to take examinations and to enter certain BHS approved competitions. Special facilities and enclosures are available to members at various events around the country.

For further information about the various departments of the BHS, their aims and the benefits for the member, consult the BHS Yearbook.

Exam Tip

The day before the examination, make sure that all riding, stable clothes and equipment are prepared. Above all relax; if possible have a hot bath in the evening and try to get a good night's sleep. Last minute revising can often cause confusion and sheer panic!

On the day, arrive at the Centre a little early if possible; there is nothing worse than being flustered and agitated through rushing or arriving late.

During the Horse Knowledge sessions take a little time over doing the practical tasks. Not too much or you will appear slow, but do not rush; yielding to the temptation to get the job over and done with quickly. It is all too easy to make silly mistakes. Be confident and sure - but not over-confident.

If, at any time, the examiner offers you advice or a different point of view, do not collapse thinking this is an automatic failure - be attentive and listen. Some emphasis is placed on the attitude of the candidate, whether or not they are willing to learn.

Remember the examiners want you to pass, they will assist and help as much as they can.

Good Luck!

APPENDIX

Recommended Series of Lectures/Practical Sessions

This recommended series of lectures and practical stable management sessions reinforce the information already given. Whilst much can be learnt from a book there really is no viable alternative to practical experience in horsemastership, no substitute for the 'hands on' method.

1   Psychology

- Psychology

  Discuss the horse's natural lifestyle, his instincts and characteristics. Discover how these are adapted and used to encourage the horse to conform to the handler's needs and requirements. Discuss the horse's body language and observe horses in the field and stable.

- Handling horses.

  Discuss working around horses correctly and safely in stable and field, the lifting of weights and performing simple stable tasks.

2   Physiology & Health

- Physiology.

  Name the points of the horse. Observe the colours and markings on several horses and ponies.

- Health.

  Discuss the signs of good and ill health. Observe some horses and assess their condition. Talk about the importance of when and why a report should be made when a horse is ill.

3   Routines

- Routines

  Discuss the importance of routines for stabled horses and those at pasture.

- Stable Equipment.

  Discuss the purpose and care of stable equipment.

- Grooming.

  Talk about methods and reasons for grooming. Study each item in a grooming kit and discuss its correct use, cleaning and storage. Groom a horse.

4   Headcollars

- Headcollars

  Discuss headcollars, halters, lead ropes, where and how to tie up a horse in the stable, yard and field. Put on a headcollar and lead rope, discuss the fit. Stand a horse up correctly and hold for treatment by the Vet or Blacksmith.

- Leading In Hand.

  Lead and turn a horse correctly at walk and trot in hand. Put on tack and practise leading a horse with and without a martingale.

- Turning The Horse Out To Grass.

  Lead a horse correctly to the field and turn him out. Catch a horse or pony in the field and bring him in.

5   Hay

- Hay

  Discuss the different methods of feeding hay, their advantages and disadvantages. Fill, weigh and tie up a haynet correctly. Discuss the different types of hay.

- Bedding.

  Discuss the principles, types, advantages and disadvantages of bedding; the methods and reasons for laying down a day and night bed. Learn to muck out, skip out, set fair a stable and yard.

- Muck Heaps.

  Discuss the principles of muck heaps; their situation in relation to the stables; their maintenance and disposal.

6   Watering and Feeding

- Watering

  Discuss the importance of water, the principles and rules of watering. Assess different types of watering systems in the stable and at grass, discussing their advantages and disadvantages.

- Feeding.

  Study some food samples, observing the different types and their quality. Discuss the basic properties of each food type and under what circumstances these would be fed. Discuss the principles and rules of feeding and the amounts of feed an average horse in light and medium work would need.

7   Saddlery

- Snaffle Bridle.

  Learn the points of the bridle. Strip a bridle, clean and reassemble. Know the different types of snaffle bits. Put a bridle on a horse and fit correctly.

- Saddle.

  Learn the points of a saddle. Put on a saddle and discuss the fitting and condition. Know the differences between a General Purpose, a Dressage and a Jumping saddle. Put on and fit a numnah/saddle cloth and discuss the advantages and disadvantages of both. Discuss the care, cleaning, and storage of saddlery. Recognize worn and ill fitting tack.

8   Clothing

Discuss the different types of rugs, uses, fitting, cleaning and storage. Put on and remove a variety of rugs with and without a roller and assess the fit.

Roll up and put on a tail bandage. Talk about its uses and care.

9   Shoeing

Study the basic structure of a horse's foot. Discuss the reasons for shoeing and the points to look for in a newly shod foot. Make a practical study from a variety of horses' feet, discussing the state of the shoes and recognizing whether or not a horse needs shoeing. Inspect some common shoe types. Talk to the Farrier.

10   Grassland Management

Assess some fields, discussing quality of pasture, size, watering systems, types of fencing, gates, shelter, danger areas, poisonous plants. Discuss the daily inspection of pasture and how to recognize a 'horse-sick' field.

11   Safety and Fire Precautions

Talk about safety in the yard, in the stable, in the fields, out on hacks and on the public highway. Discuss fire precautions, types and localities of extinguishers and procedures in case of fire. Discuss the procedures for accidents in the yard, when hacking or whilst riding on the roads, basic first aid and how and where to get help. Talk about the country code.

12   General

Discuss the aims of the British Horse Society. Revise any sections necessary. Discuss examination techniques, clothing and other requirements.

During these sessions or in a 'mock' exam, practise having questions fired at you so that you learn to answer quickly and clearly.

To help with the studying, design your own timetable that suits your lifestyle. Perhaps taking in a chapter per week divided into theory and practical sessions.

Index